Magic BEANS

150 DELICIOUS RECIPES FEATURING

NATURE'S LOW-FAT, NUTRIENT-RICH, DISEASE-FIGHTING POWERHOUSE

PATTI BAZEL GEIL,
M.S., R.D., C.D.E.

JOHN WILEY & SONS, INC.

New York • Chichester • Weinheim • Brisbane • Singapore • Toronto

Copyright © 1996 by Patti Bazel Geil. All rights reserved
Published by John Wiley & Sons, Inc.
Published simultaneously in Canada
Previously published by Chronimed Publishing

Illustrations: Joe Heffron

The information contained in this book is not intended to serve as a replacement for professional medical advice. Any use of the information in this book is at the reader's discretion. The author and the publisher specifically disclaim any and all liability arising directly or indirectly from the use or application of any information contained in this book. A health care professional should be consulted regarding your specific situation.

Library of Congress Cataloging-in-Publication Data:

ISBN 0-471-34747-7

Printed in the United States of America

10   9   8   7   6   5

Acknowledgments

Many thanks to the family, friends, and nutrition professionals who tasted, tested, and encouraged me during the writing of this book. Special appreciation to my husband, Jack, for his endless technical and moral support, and to Kristen and Rachel, my littlest bean eaters!

Contents

Introduction
vii

. . . .

About the Recipes
ix

. . . .

If You Don't Know Beans...
1

. . . .

"Beaning" Up on the Health Benefits
9

. . . .

Using the Old Bean
13

. . . .

Bean Cuisine
Appetizers
19

. . . .

Souped Up Beans
Soups & Chilis
41

. . . .

Beans and Greens

Salads

65

. . . .

Full of Beans

Main Dishes

99

. . . .

Baked Beans & Beyond

Side Dishes

151

. . . .

Brave-Hearted Bean Lover

Unique Bean Recipes

175

. . . .

Bibliography

183

. . . .

Index

185

. . . .

Introduction

I learned something when I began writing this cookbook—people think beans are a funny food. Whenever I told anyone about my cookbook of 150 bean recipes, I usually heard one of several comments, following the suppressed giggles:

"I know beans are good for me, but don't they take all day to cook?"

"What can you do with them besides make baked beans?"

And the inevitable "I like beans, but they don't like me," a delicate way of bringing up the subject of flatulence!

My purpose in writing *Magic Beans* is to address these concerns and provide recipes for today's cooks—recipes that are tasty, convenient, and nutritionally sound.

Remember the fairy tale of *Jack and the Beanstalk*? According to legend, Jack, a poor peasant boy, infuriated his mother by trading their precious cow for a handful of colored beans. Jack may have made his mother angry, but he did make a very smart nutrition move by trading his cow—a source of high fat, high cholesterol, and high saturated fat foods such as milk and beef—for nature's nutrition powerhouse, dry beans. These tiny wonders are low fat, nutrient-rich, and delicious besides!

During my career as a registered dietitian, I've yet to find a food with more nutritional advantages than dry beans. As Chapter 2 outlines, beans have the perfect nutrients to assist in weight loss, control of diabetes mellitus, lowering of high cholesterol, cancer prevention, and improved functioning of the gastrointestinal tract. Beans are low in fat and cholesterol, yet rich in complex carbohydrate, fiber, vitamins, and minerals.

Obviously, no one can eat beans three meals a day, seven days a week. However, I hope readers will browse through this book, selecting new recipes to try on a regular basis. By including two or three bean dishes a week in your diet, the difference in your health—and food budget—will soon become apparent. Break down your bean barriers and begin enjoying the great taste of one of nature's most perfect foods.

"Bean" There Done That

As *Magic Beans* will show, it's almost impossible to overstate the benefits of eating beans, both nutritionally and in terms of taste. To summarize the benefits in the style of a well-known late night talk show host:

Top Ten Reasons To Eat Beans:

10. They're economical.

9. They're versatile.

8. They're low in fat.

7. They're high in fiber.

6. They're low in sodium.

5. They're a great source of vitamins and minerals.

4. They're packed with protein.

3. They're delicious in ethnic dishes.

2. They're convenient.

1. They taste great!

This is by no means an all-inclusive bean cookbook. Different varieties of beans abound. In fact, I found it difficult to stay within the limit of the 150 recipes needed for this book. My files are brimming with additional quick, convenient, and tasty ways to enjoy the nutritional benefits of beans. If you have favorite bean recipes or tips for using beans, please send them to me: Patti Bazel Geil, c/o Chronimed Publishing, 13911 Ridgedale Drive, Minnetonka, MN 55305. We have the potential to perform more bean magic. *Bean appetit!*

Magic BEANS

About the Recipes

"In cooking, as in all the arts, simplicity is the sign of perfection."
—Curnonsky

"Successful cooks do as little as possible to achieve whatever desired results."
— Alan Koehler

The recipes in this book were chosen to meet three basic criteria: tasty, convenient, and nutritionally sound. Some of the recipes were created as adaptations of high-fat versions of traditional dishes. Others came from family, friends, nutrition professionals, and clients. Still others were inspired by those I found during my years researching nutrition and beans. All of the recipes in this book have been carefully tested by me, family, friends, or nutrition professionals. Most take less than 30 minutes to put together or require minimum "hands on" preparation time. The cooking time may take longer but doesn't demand the cook's full attention in the kitchen.

This is not intended to be a vegetarian cookbook, but many of the recipes are suitable for plant-centered diets. All of the recipes are low in fat, saturated fat, and cholesterol. When part of a balanced day's diet, they fall within the recommendation of no more than 20-30% of total calories from fat. Some of the dessert recipes do contain added sugar, which should be accounted for in the diet of a person with diabetes. Most of the recipes in this book are based on canned beans for the sake of convenience; however, when time is available, I encourage preparing dry beans from scratch particularly if budget and sodium are of concern. When using canned beans, rinsing the beans in cool water and draining them is recommended to keep sodium content as low as possible. Chapter 3 contains helpful hints on preparing dry beans with conversion charts showing the amount of dry beans to substitute for canned.

Nutrient analysis of recipes was performed using Nutritionist IV for Windows, Diet Analysis Module, Version 3.5 (First DataBank, N-Squared Computing, The Hearst Corporation, 1111 Bayhill Drive, San Bruno, CA 94066). Food exchange information is based on the 1995 Exchange Lists for Meal Planning (The American Dietetic Association and The American Diabetes Association).

If You Don't Know Beans...

1

"And God said: Behold I have given you every herb-bearing seed upon the earth, and all the trees that have in themselves seed of their own kind, to be your meat."— Genesis 1:29

Beans are one of our oldest foods, dating back to Biblical times. Ancient civilizations cultivated them and held them in high regard. In fact, the names of the four most prominent families in Rome were derived from each of the major legumes known to Romans: Fabius from the fava bean; Lentulus from the lentil; Piso from the pea; and Cicero from the chickpea. Fava beans were used in elections in ancient Rome—white beans meaning "for" and black "against." Early cultures held bean festivals to honor Apollo, offered up beans to the dead at wakes, and built temples to beans as a symbol of respect. All of this adoration was taking place long before modern nutrition scientists discovered the many health benefits of beans!

Bean Basics

What makes beans so special? The answer lies deep within their colorful seed coats. Beans are members of the legume family, the third largest family of flowering plants and the second most important in the human diet. Legumes, also known as pulses, are characterized by seed-bearing pods. They may appear quite different from one another in color and shape, depending on the species. Surprisingly, peanuts are technically not nuts, but are considered to be members of the legume family as are soybeans, another pulse grown for both oil and protein content. Think of creamy white oval navy beans, deep red kidney-shaped kidney beans, green or red lens-shaped lentils. Although they may not resemble each other on the outside, their interior structure is remarkably alike.

Beans are nutrition powerhouses. They are self-contained packets of the proteins, carbohydrates, fats, vitamins, and minerals needed to sustain a plant until it is able to survive on its own. In addition, beans are environmentally-friendly. They absorb nitrogen from the air, turn it into compounds that can be used by the plant, and enrich the soil when they decay.

The Inside Story

An alphabet soup of good nutrition is packed into dry beans. Here's the inside story:

Nutrition breakdown for Navy Beans, 1/2 cup serving, cooked

Calories 130
Protein . . . . .8 G.
Carbohydrate . . . . .24 G.
Total Fiber . . . . .6.5 G.
Soluble Fiber . . . . .2.2 G.
Fat .0.5 G.
   Saturated Fat . . . .<1 G.
   Cholesterol . . . . .0 MG.

Vitamins
   Folic Acid . . . . .128 MCG.
   Thiamin . . . . .0.2 MG.
   Pyridoxine . . . . .0.2 MG.
   Niacin . . . . .0.5 MG.
   Riboflavin . . . . .0.1 MG.

Minerals
   Sodium . . . . .1 MG.
   Iron . . . . .2.3 MG.
   Phosphorus . . . . .143 MG.
   Magnesium . . . . .54 MG.
   Manganese . . . . .0.5 MG.
   Potassium . . . . .335 MG.
   Copper . . . . .0.3 MG.
   Calcium . . . . .64 MG.
   Zinc . . . . .1 MG.

Calories: 1/2 cup of cooked, dry beans provides 110 to 145 calories, depending on the variety of bean. Most of the energy in beans comes from complex carbohydrate, also known as starch.

Protein: Beans have long been known as an economical source of protein; in fact, they are sometimes called "poor man's meat." Because beans are plants,

Magic BEANS

their fat, saturated fat, and cholesterol content is minimal. For those of us concerned with good health, this makes beans a real nutrition bargain in the protein department. Ten grams of protein from navy beans (2.7 ounces, uncooked) costs a miserly 8 cents and supplies less than a gram of either fat or saturated fat. In comparison, 10 grams of protein from cheddar cheese (1.4 ounces) cost three times as much (26 cents) and dumps over 13 grams of fat and 8 grams of artery-clogging saturated fat into the bloodstream.

What is the quality of the protein in beans? Most plant-based foods, including beans and grains, do not contain the complete profile of essential amino acids needed for good health. The exception is soybeans, which have a protein value equal to animal-based proteins such as meat, milk, and eggs. Fortunately, when other complementary foods such as grains or corn are eaten the same day as beans, the quality of the protein and its usefulness to the body increase. Many tasty bean dishes achieve this goal naturally—think of black beans and rice, Hoppin' John, or corn tortillas and beans!

Carbohydrate: Complex carbohydrate is the main component of dry beans. This makes beans a perfect food to emphasize in a meal plan to meet the current nutrition recommendations to eat more grains, starches, vegetables, and fruits. Beans also contain small amounts of sugar, notably oligosaccharides such as the alpha-galactosides. Humans lack the enzyme needed to digest these bean sugars, causing the gas that plagues certain bean-eaters. Chapter 3 gives some practical advice on beating the bean bloat.

Fiber: Few foods beat beans as a source of dietary fiber, both the insoluble fiber that improves the function of the gastrointestinal tract and soluble fiber which lowers blood cholesterol and helps regulate blood sugar. It would take 4 slices of whole wheat bread to match the total fiber in 1/2 cup of navy beans, and over 7 slices to equal the soluble fiber content! Only oats and certain high fiber cereals come close to packing the same high fiber punch as beans. Chapter 2 details the importance of fiber—and beans—in fighting disease.

Fat: Because beans are plants, they are naturally low in fat and saturated fat, and are cholesterol-free. Most beans have less than 1 gram of total fat per serving, making them ideal to serve as an entree in meatless meals. The exceptions are soybeans, which have 7 grams of fat per 1/2 cup serving, and peanuts, which are loaded with 36 grams of fat per 1/2 cup. As Chapter 2 notes, lowering fat, saturated fat, and cholesterol intake is a key part of the current dietary advice to help reduce the risk for chronic diseases such as diabetes mellitus, heart disease, cancer, and obesity. Beans are the perfect food to include in the diet to meet these recommendations.

Vitamins: Beans are a delicious way to satisfy crucial vitamin requirements. They are good sources of water-soluble vitamins such as folacin, thiamin, pyridoxine, riboflavin, and niacin. In fact, a 1 cup serving of cooked dry beans can provide 25% of the adult US Recommended Dietary Allowance (RDA) for thiamin, 10-12% of pyridoxine, and about 10% of the required riboflavin and niacin. Women of child-bearing age should be especially concerned about their intake of folacin, because maternal folacin deficiency has been associated with birth defects. The adult RDA for folacin is 180 mcg, and the Public Health Service recommends that women of child-bearing age consume 400 mcg of folacin daily. A 1 cup serving of cooked navy beans provides 256 mcg of folacin in a tasty, low fat, high fiber package.

Minerals: Calcium, iron, copper, zinc, phosphorus, potassium, and magnesium are a few of the minerals found in substantial amounts in beans. A 1 cup serving of cooked dry beans provides 29% of the RDA for iron for females and 55% for males, 20-25% of phosphorus and magnesium, 20% of potassium and copper, and 10% of the required calcium and zinc. Dry beans are naturally very low in sodium, which must often be carefully limited by people with hypertension, kidney disease, and cardiac conditions. A 1 cup serving of cooked dry navy beans contains a slim 2 mg of sodium; however, the same amount of canned navy beans serves up a significant 1173 mg of sodium. Rinse canned beans under cool water for at least 1 minute and drain to reduce the sodium content by up to 40%.

Magic BEANS

A User-Friendly Guide to Beans

"If ever there was a staple food in need of a good public relations campaign, it's the hapless bean." Sheryl and Mel London, authors of *The Versatile Grain and the Elegant Bean*

Although many people know beans are wonderful food for good health, beans have an undeserved reputation as time-consuming and difficult to prepare. While a good public relations campaign would certainly help beans, this cookbook has been designed to help overcome bean barriers and highlight the many delicious, convenient, and nutritional ways to fix these proven powerhouses. To know beans is to love them! The following chart introduces the most common beans and provides descriptions and serving suggestions for each.

The Best of the Beans

Black (turtle beans)
- Black-skinned ovals
- A staple in South American and Caribbean dishes

Black-eyed peas (cowpeas)
- Creamy skin with dark dot
- Southern dishes, Hoppin' John

Cannellini
- Small white ovals
- Italian cuisine

Fava
- Large, beige with wrinkled skin
- Mediterranean cuisine

Garbanzo (chickpea, ceci)
- Round, beige, nut-like
- Middle Eastern cuisine

Great Northern
- Large white ovals
- Soups, stews, baked beans

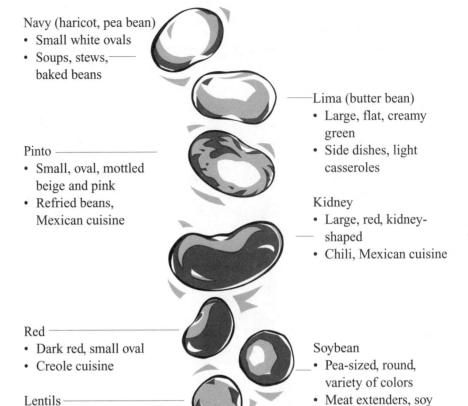

Navy (haricot, pea bean)
- Small white ovals
- Soups, stews, —— baked beans

Lima (butter bean)
- Large, flat, creamy green
- Side dishes, light casseroles

Pinto ————
- Small, oval, mottled beige and pink
- Refried beans, Mexican cuisine

Kidney
- Large, red, kidney-shaped
- Chili, Mexican cuisine

Red ————
- Dark red, small oval
- Creole cuisine

Soybean
- Pea-sized, round, variety of colors
- Meat extenders, soy sauce, tofu

Lentils ————
- Small, lens-shaped, red or green
- Soups, casseroles

Magic BEANS

Bean Tidbits

Because of their nutritional similarities, mild taste, and ability to absorb the flavors in which they are cooked, beans can often be interchanged for one another in recipes. What can't be exchanged, however, is the unique history and lore associated with each legume. Here are some uncommon tidbits about common beans:

Black beans have a rich, earthy taste and soft texture. A South American staple, they are becoming more popular in the United States in dishes such as soups, salads, and dips with a Southwest flavor.

Black-eyed peas are thin-skinned and may be cooked without pre-soaking. Available in dry, canned, or frozen form.

Cannellini beans have a smooth texture and subtle, nutty flavor. Although originally cultivated in Argentina, they are now grown in Italy and associated with its cuisine.

Fava beans were forbidden by the followers of the ancient philosopher Pythagoras, who thought they contained the souls of the dead. Favism is a rare genetic disease in which susceptible individuals develop acute anemia after eating fava beans.

Garbanzo beans, one of the most versatile of all the legumes, are extremely hard and require long pre-soaking time. Hummus is a popular bean paste made from garbanzo beans.

Great Northern beans are from the haricot family and are the largest beans in the white bean family. They are often used in soups, stews, and the French stew, cassoulet.

Kidney beans are an all-purpose favorite and can be found in recipes from appetizers to desserts. Their distinctive kidney shape adds eye appeal to many dishes.

Lentils need no soaking and cook relatively quickly; they are considered the "fast food" of the legume family. They are grown in a concentrated area near Washington and Idaho; historically, up to 80% of the crops have been exported.

Lima beans come in two varieties—baby and large. They are natives of Central America and were named for the capital of Peru. Lima beans were staples in the American Indian diet.

Navy beans are the mature, dried white seed of the green bean and are probably the most widely used of beans. They appear in dishes ranging from Boston Baked Beans to soups and salads.

Pinto beans are prime ingredients of Tex-Mex dishes. Their name is derived from the Spanish word for "painted" due to their mottled appearance, which turns into a uniform pink when cooked.

Red beans are related to kidney beans and are used in much the same way. They are the unique ingredient in the traditional New Orleans dish, red beans and rice.

Soybeans are higher in protein and fat than most other beans. They are not often soaked and used in cooking outside of China and Japan, yet are frequently consumed in the United States in the form of margarine, meat extenders, and tofu.

"Beaning" Up on the Health Benefits

Beans have long been associated with magic: from ancient fortune tellers who used beans to predict the future, to the offerings of legumes that superstitious Greeks made to Apollo in hopes of a good harvest. But nowhere is the magic of beans more potent than in today's fight against the chronic diseases that contribute to the leading causes of death in the United States—coronary heart disease, diabetes mellitus, obesity, and cancer.

The Dietary Guidelines for Americans include seven suggestions for a healthful diet to reduce the risk of certain diseases. Beans fill the bill by helping consumers meet six of those recommendations:

- Eat a variety of foods.
- Balance the food you eat with physical activity—maintain or improve your weight.
- Choose a diet with plenty of grain products, vegetables, and fruits.
- Choose a diet low in fat, saturated fat, and cholesterol.
- Choose a diet moderate in sugars.
- Choose a diet moderate in salt and sodium.
- If you drink alcoholic beverages, do so in moderation.

The Benefits Of Beans

A healthy diet is crucial to lowering the risk factors for coronary heart disease, particularly elevated blood cholesterol. Beans are naturally low in fat and rich in soluble fiber, which possesses proven cholesterol-lowering effects. Beans are particularly effective in those people whose blood cholesterol levels are highest. In several studies in which people ate a variety of dry beans in amounts ranging from 1/3 cup to 1 cup daily, blood cholesterol was lowered an average of 9.7% after 3 weeks. Canned beans are also effective.

In a number of research studies, daily consumption of canned beans lowered total cholesterol an average of 11.7% after 3 weeks. Protein from soybeans is proven to lower total cholesterol, as well as the "bad" low-density lipoprotein (LDL) cholesterol. Just a 1% decrease in serum cholesterol results in a 2% decrease in the risk of coronary heart disease, so even the smallest change can reap significant results.

Beans also make a difference in diets for individuals with diabetes. Beans are generally digested slowly and produce a low rise in blood glucose. This means less insulin or oral hypoglycemic agent is needed to complete the metabolism of beans. An added bonus is the improvement in blood fat levels and improved heart health that comes from eating beans. People with diabetes are at three to four times more risk for heart attacks and strokes than people without diabetes.

One out of every four Americans suffers from obesity, which increases their chance for coronary heart disease, high blood pressure, and diabetes. Research has shown that including beans as part of a weight loss plan delays the return of hunger after a meal and helps people feel full longer. Although Americans spend over $30 billion annually on diet programs and products, the economical bean is probably the most cost-effective ally in the battle of the bulge.

Cancer is the second leading cause of death in this country, and eight of ten types of cancer are related to diet. Large-scale studies show that beans may decrease the risk of colon cancer by speeding the passage of food through the gastrointestinal tract, taking with it potential cancer-causing compounds and minimizing the exposure time of cells. Soybeans contain a variety of compounds known as phytochemicals, which have great potential in preventing cancer.

The nutrient composition of beans enables them to provide health benefits in a way matched by very few other foods. As mentioned earlier, beans provide protein, complex carbohydrate, fiber, and essential vitamins and minerals, yet are low in total fat, saturated fat, and sodium, and contain no cholesterol. However, phytochemicals may be the magic ingredients that give beans the reputation as "gourmet preventive medicine." Much excitement has been generated recently over phytochemicals. These naturally occurring compounds may enable a plant food to have even more health-promoting potential than is due to its nutritional makeup alone. Soybeans have at least four phytochemicals associated with reduced risk of colon, breast, and ovarian cancer. Broccoli, onions, and garlic are also rich in phytochemicals. Further research

Magic BEANS

into their effect may prove exactly why eating more vegetables, fruit, grains, seeds, and legumes reduces the risk of cancer.

Pyramid Power

The Dietary Guidelines for Americans advise eating more fruits, vegetables, and grains while reducing intake of calories, fat, saturated fat, cholesterol, and sodium. Beans are just what the doctor and dietitian ordered to meet these recommendations. In fact, beans are such nutrition powerhouses that they have been placed in two categories on the USDA Food Pyramid Guide: the vegetable group and as inexpensive alternatives for lean meat, poultry, and fish in the meat group. No matter where they're placed on the pyramid, beans belong in everyone's meal plan.

Food Pyramid Guide

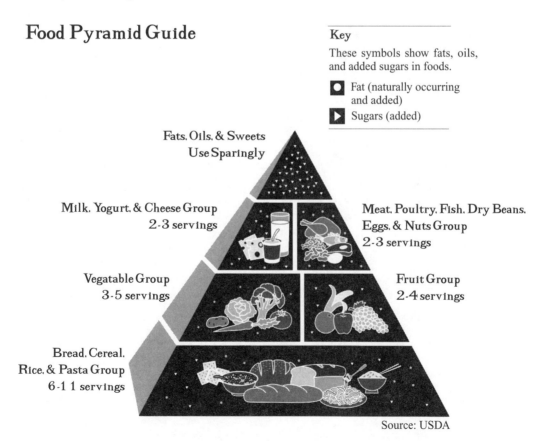

Key

These symbols show fats, oils, and added sugars in foods.

○ Fat (naturally occurring and added)

▶ Sugars (added)

Fats, Oils, & Sweets
Use Sparingly

Milk, Yogurt, & Cheese Group
2-3 servings

Meat, Poultry, Fish, Dry Beans,
Eggs, & Nuts Group
2-3 servings

Vegatable Group
3-5 servings

Fruit Group
2-4 servings

Bread, Cereal,
Rice, & Pasta Group
6-11 servings

Source: USDA

Using the Old Bean

3

Beans are one of nature's most perfect foods: low in fat, packed with nutrition, and a strong ally in the fight against chronic disease. But that all amounts to a hill of beans if the beans don't get eaten! Here are some tips for shopping for, cooking with, and storing beans.

Shopping

From exotic to common, an almost endless selection of legumes is available in a variety of places such as health food stores, ethnic specialty shops, mail order catalogs, and the corner grocery store. Beans are sold in bulk, in bags, in cans, and, in the case of lima beans and black-eyed peas, in the freezer. If budget is an issue, bulk and bagged beans are usually the most inexpensive; if you use canned beans, you pay for the convenience. Buy the freshest beans you can find, because beans that have been stored for an extended time harden and are difficult to cook.

Cooking

Cooking with beans is as easy as 1, 2, 3: rinsing, soaking, and cooking.

Rinsing: Rinse beans and lentils before soaking and cooking to remove dust and any visible debris.

Soaking: Dry beans must be soaked before cooking to return the moisture that was lost through processing to the bean. Soaking also reduces cooking time, removes much of the bean sugar that causes flatulence, and improves the bean's texture and appearance. Exceptions to the rule are lentils, split peas, and black-eyed peas, which are thin-skinned and may be cooked without soaking.

Traditional soaking method- Place beans in a large pot. Add 6 cups of cold water for each pound of dry beans. Soak beans overnight, then drain and discard soaking water. Rinse, drain, and cook.

Quick soaking method- Place beans in a large pot. Add 6 to 8 cups of hot water for each pound of dry beans. Heat the water to boiling and cook for 2 minutes. Turn off the heat, cover the pot, and let beans stand for 1 hour. Rinse, drain, and cook.

Extra-quick soaking method- Place beans in a large pot. Cover with 2 inches of water. Bring to a boil. Reduce heat to medium and let boil 10 minutes. Drain beans, then cover with 2 inches of fresh cool water. Let soak 30 minutes. Rinse, drain, and cook.

Extra-extra quick soaking method- Skip the soaking step altogether by using canned beans, which many of the recipes in this cookbook allow. Remember to rinse and drain the beans before cooking to remove excess sodium.

Cooking: Should beans be cooked in their soaking water? Using the water again preserves the small amount of vitamins and protein that may have escaped into the soaking water. However, the soaking water also contains the sugars that can produce gas. Because beans have nutrients to spare, the best bet is to discard the soaking water and pass on the gas.

After soaking, most varieties of beans will need additional cooking to become fully tender and ready to eat or be used in a recipe. To cook, add seasoning and additional water; simmer for approximately 2 hours or until beans are tender. Remember, many bean recipes include the cooking time for beans as part of the total cooking time, so review the recipe carefully and take this into consideration.

Beans can also be cooked in a pressure cooker, microwave, or Crockpot.

A pressure cooker will cook soaked dry beans thoroughly in as little as 15 to 20 minutes. Be careful to follow manufacturer's directions, avoid overfilling the pot, and cook with no more than 10 to 15 pounds of pressure. Adding approximately 1 tablespoon of vegetable oil to the beans before cooking will prevent them from foaming and bubbling up through the pressure valve.

Using a microwave to cook beans has pros and cons. While the microwave is handy for reheating cooked or canned beans and thawing frozen beans, many food experts feel that dry beans should be simmered slowly in plenty of water to preserve their full flavor. To soak beans in the microwave, place 1 pound of beans and 8 cups of water in a large glass casserole dish. Cover and cook on high for 8 to 10 minutes or until boiling. Let stand for 1 hour, stirring occasionally. To cook dry beans in the microwave, add 6 to 8 cups of hot water to

Magic BEANS

1 pound of soaked beans. Cover and cook at high for 8 to 10 minutes or until boiling. Stir and cook at medium for another 15 to 20 minutes or until beans are tender. Stir again, then let stand 5 minutes to complete cooking.

A Crockpot is ideal for cooking beans because it gives them a chance to absorb the flavor of a recipe by simmering slowly in a blend of herbs and spices. Follow manufacturer's or recipe directions carefully. To cook beans alone, place soaked beans in a saucepan with enough water to cover. Bring to a boil, reduce heat, and simmer for 10 minutes. Discard the water and place beans in the crockpot. Add 6 cups of water for each pound of beans to be cooked. Cook on low setting for 6 to 12 hours or until beans are tender.

Cooking with lentils and split peas: Because lentils and split peas are thin skinned, cooking with them is a bit different than cooking with dry beans. Remember . . . don't soak, don't soak, don't soak! To cook, use twice the amount of liquid as with split peas or lentils. Combine lentils or split peas and liquid in a saucepan. Cover; bring to a boil. Reduce heat and simmer 15 minutes for salad recipes, 30 minutes for vegetable and main dish recipes, and 45 minutes for soups and purees. Lentils and split peas can be cooked in a microwave, but pressure cooking is not advised.

Storage

Beans can be stored almost indefinitely if placed in a tightly covered container in a dry place. Cooked beans should be covered, then refrigerated up to 4 to 5 days. Cooked beans and bean dishes can be frozen in covered containers up to 6 months. Freeze cooked beans in Ziplock bags in 1-cup portions; thaw and use in favorite recipes.

A Bag Of Bean Cooking Tips

- Most experienced cooks don't add baking soda to their beans to speed the cooking process unless their water is extremely hard. If that is the case, add no more than 1/8 teaspoon of baking soda per cup of beans. Too much baking soda reduces the nutritional value and flavor of beans.

- Acid slows the bean tenderizing process. Don't add acid food ingredients such as tomatoes, lemon juice, vinegar, or wine to beans until they are nearly tender. Adding salt to beans during soaking or too early during cooking will also toughen the seed coat and prevent the absorption of liquid. Again, wait until the beans are nearly tender to add salt if needed.

- Chili powders, coriander, cumin, thyme, and oregano are spices that blend well with all varieties of beans.

- Cook double batches of beans whenever possible. Freezing the leftovers saves soaking and cooking time in the future.

Bean Counting

- Dry beans triple in volume when soaked and cooked.

  1 pound dry beans = 2 cups uncooked beans

  1 cup dry beans = 3 cups soaked and cooked

  1 pound or 2 cups dry beans = 6 cups soaked and cooked

  1 pound lentils = 2 1/3 cups uncooked lentils

- One cup of dry beans, soaked and cooked, serves four people as a side dish or as part of a main dish when combined with other ingredients.

- Canned beans, rinsed and drained, are a quick and convenient substitute for cooked beans in favorite recipes.

  15- to 16-ounce can of beans = 2 cups soaked and cooked dry beans

  15- to 16-ounce can of beans = 1 2/3 cup canned beans

In Search Of The Social Bean

"Vegetarianism is harmless enough, though it is apt to fill a man with wind and self-righteousness." —Sir Robert Hutchinson

"Beans, beans they're good for your heart, the more you eat the more . . ." We all know the end to that childhood nursery rhyme. Despite the bountiful health benefits of beans, many people won't eat them because of their gas-producing effect. This can be traced to the small amount of complex sugars in beans, called alpha-galactosides. Since humans lack alpha-galactosidase, the enzyme necessary to digest these sugars, the bacteria in the lower intestine break them down, producing gas. To beat the bean bloat:

Magic BEANS

- Proper soaking and cooking can rid beans of up to 90% of their gas-producing potential. Use the quick soaking method described earlier, changing the soaking water as frequently as possible. The boiling process softens the bean skin, allowing the offending sugars to leach more readily into the water. Don't cook beans in their soaking water since that's where the gas-producing sugars hide. In Mexico, beans are traditionally prepared with epazote, a pungent herb that is said to counteract the indigestible sugars.

- Drain and rinse canned beans thoroughly to rid them of a portion of the gas-producing sugar as well as excess sodium.

- Lentils, black-eyed peas, lima beans, garbanzo beans, and white beans are considered by some people to be "less gassy."

- Don't jump on the "bean wagon" full blast. If you're not used to eating beans, start gradually by adding 1/2 cup servings of legumes 1 or 2 times per week. Beans are most problematic for people who don't eat them often.

- Chew beans thoroughly and drink adequate amounts of fluid to aid their digestion.

- Beano® is a liquid alpha-galactosidase preparation that has been proven to lower the incidence of intestinal complaints after eating beans. According to manufacturer's directions, a few drops mixed with the "offending food" is all that's needed. Beano can be found in most grocery stores and pharmacies.

- Genetic engineering may lead the way to the final solution in the search for a "social" bean. Researchers are developing varieties of gasless beans, which have been genetically altered so they are naturally lower in gas-producing sugars.

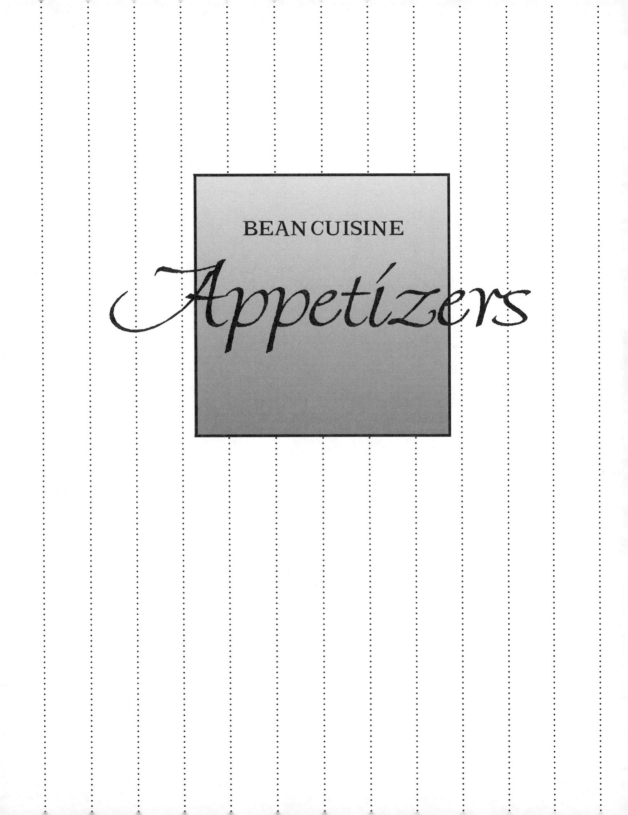

BEAN CUISINE

Appetizers

Faux Caviar

This is almost as good as the real thing! Serve with baked tortilla chips or pita bread triangles.

2 15-ounce cans black-eyed peas, rinsed and drained
4-ounce can mushrooms, drained and diced
1 medium onion, finely diced
2 tablespoons Italian seasoning
1/2 cup fat-free Italian salad dressing
1 tablespoon diced green chiles, drained
1 small red pepper, diced
1 teaspoon black pepper

Mix all ingredients. Chill overnight.

PREPARATION TIME:
15 MINUTES

CHILLING TIME:
8 HOURS

NUTRIENT INFORMATION
(PER SERVING):
SERVINGS PER RECIPE: 64
SERVING SIZE: 1 TABLESPOON
CALORIES   33
PROTEIN   2 G.
CARBOHYDRATE   5 G.
FAT   1 G.
SATURATED FAT   < 1 G.
CHOLESTEROL   0 MG.
SODIUM   42 MG.
DIETARY FIBER   2 G.

% CALORIES FROM:
PROTEIN: 24%
CARBOHYDRATE: 61%
FAT: 15%

FOOD EXCHANGES:
1 VEGETABLE

MAKES 4 CUPS.

Take-Five Dip

PREPARATION TIME:
5 MINUTES

NUTRIENT INFORMATION
(PER SERVING):
SERVINGS PER RECIPE: 24
SERVING SIZE: 1 TABLESPOON
CALORIES   33
PROTEIN   2 G.
CARBOHYDRATE   5 G.
FAT   <1 G.
SATURATED FAT   <1 G.
CHOLESTEROL   <1 MG.
SODIUM   38 MG.
DIETARY FIBER   1 G.

% CALORIES FROM:
PROTEIN: 24%
CARBOHYDRATE: 61%
FAT: 15%

FOOD EXCHANGES:
1 VEGETABLE

MAKES 1 1/2 CUPS.

What could be quicker and easier than a five ingredient bean dip? Keep all five ingredients on hand for last minute company.

16-ounce can black beans, rinsed and drained

1/2 cup mild salsa

2 tablespoons fresh lime juice

2 tablespoons chopped fresh cilantro

1/4 teaspoon ground cumin

Combine all ingredients in a food processor. Process until smooth. If desired, season with salt and freshly ground black pepper.

Magic BEANS

Garbanzo Guac

Garbanzo beans replace part of the high-fat avocado in this healthy alternative to guacamole dip. Serve with toasted corn tortilla wedges.

1 cup canned garbanzo beans, rinsed and drained
1 tablespoon lemon juice
1 clove garlic, minced
3/4 cup coarsely chopped onion
1/4 cup peeled, cubed avocado
1 tablespoon diced green chiles
1/4 teaspoon salt
1/4 teaspoon cayenne pepper
3/4 cup seeded, finely chopped, unpeeled tomato
1/2 cup finely chopped green onions

Place beans, lemon juice, and garlic in a food processor. Process 20 seconds, stopping once to scrape the sides of the bowl with a rubber spatula. Add onion, avocado, green chiles, salt, and cayenne pepper. Process, pulsing 5 times or until mixture is chunky. Place mixture in a bowl, and stir in chopped tomato and green onions. Cover and chill 1 hour.

PREPARATION TIME:
10 MINUTES

CHILLING TIME:
1 HOUR

NUTRIENT INFORMATION
(PER SERVING):
SERVINGS PER RECIPE: 16
SERVING SIZE: 2 TABLESPOONS
CALORIES   33
PROTEIN   2 G.
CARBOHYDRATE   4 G.
FAT   1 G.
SATURATED FAT   <1 G.
CHOLESTEROL   0 MG.
SODIUM   102 MG.
DIETARY FIBER   1 G.

% CALORIES FROM:
PROTEIN: 24%
CARBOHYDRATE: 48%
FAT: 27%

FOOD EXCHANGES:
1 VEGETABLE

MAKES 2 CUPS.

Hummus Dip

PREPARATION TIME:
5 MINUTES

NUTRIENT INFORMATION
(PER SERVING):
SERVINGS PER RECIPE: 32
SERVING SIZE: 1 TABLESPOON
CALORIES   25
PROTEIN   1 G.
CARBOHYDRATE   4 G.
FAT   <1 G.
SATURATED FAT   < 1 G.
CHOLESTEROL   0 MG.
SODIUM   129 MG.
DIETARY FIBER   1 G.

% CALORIES FROM:
PROTEIN: 16%
CARBOHYDRATE: 64%
FAT: 20%

FOOD EXCHANGES:
1 VEGETABLE

MAKES 2 CUPS.

Tahini is a thick paste made from ground sesame seeds, which can be found in the ethnic section of major supermarkets, Middle Eastern markets, or health food stores. It's worth looking for to use this tasty recipe!

16-ounce can garbanzo beans
2 tablespoons tahini
1 tablespoon lemon juice
1 teaspoon salt
1 clove garlic
1/2 teaspoon ground cumin

Drain garbanzo beans, reserving liquid. Place all ingredients in a food processor. Process until smooth. Add reserved liquid from garbanzo beans until desired dipping consistency is reached. Serve with toasted bite-sized triangles of pita bread.

Magic BEANS

Down-Home Hummus

Black-eyed peas give a "down-home" taste to this variation of the traditional Middle Eastern spread. Serve with crackers or breadsticks.

15-ounce can black-eyed peas, undrained
3 green onions, sliced
1 clove garlic
2 tablespoons diced green chiles
4 sprigs fresh cilantro
1/2 cup tahini*
3 tablespoons lemon juice
1/2 teaspoon salt
1/4 teaspoon ground cumin

Drain black-eyed peas, reserving liquid. Place all ingredients except reserved liquid in a food processor. Process until smooth. Add reserved liquid until desired spreading consistency is reached.

PREPARATION TIME:
5 MINUTES

NUTRIENT INFORMATION
(PER SERVING):
SERVINGS PER RECIPE: 28
SERVING SIZE: 1 TABLESPOON
CALORIES   19
PROTEIN   <1 G.
CARBOHYDRATE   3 G.
FAT   <1 G.
SATURATED FAT   <1 G.
CHOLESTEROL   0 MG.
SODIUM   51 MG.
DIETARY FIBER   2 G.

% CALORIES FROM:
PROTEIN: 11%
CARBOHYDRATE: 63%
FAT: 26%

FOOD EXCHANGES:
1 VEGETABLE

MAKES 1 3/4 CUPS.

*Tahini is a paste made from ground sesame seeds. You'll find it in the ethnic section of major supermarkets, Middle Eastern markets, or health food stores.

Savory White Bean Dip

PREPARATION TIME:
5 MINUTES

NUTRIENT INFORMATION
(PER SERVING):
SERVINGS PER RECIPE: 32
SERVING SIZE: 1 TABLESPOON
CALORIES   25
PROTEIN   1 G.
CARBOHYDRATE   4 G.
FAT   <1 G.
SATURATED FAT   <1 G.
CHOLESTEROL   0 MG.
SODIUM   20 MG.
DIETARY FIBER   1 G.

% CALORIES FROM:
PROTEIN: 16%
CARBOHYDRATE: 64%
FAT: 20%

FOOD EXCHANGES:
1 VEGETABLE

MAKES 2 CUPS.

Try this low-fat dip with pretzels or fat-free chips.

1/2 cup fresh parsley

1/3 cup fresh cilantro

1/4 cup chopped green onions

1/2 teaspoon chili powder

1/2 teaspoon ground cumin

1/4 teaspoon salt

1/4 teaspoon crushed coriander

1/4 teaspoon black pepper

1/2 teaspoon paprika

2 cloves garlic

2 tablespoons fresh lemon juice

1 tablespoon plain nonfat yogurt

15-ounce can cannellini beans, rinsed and drained

Place all ingredients in a food processor or blender. Process until smooth.

Magic BEANS

Appetizer Black Bean Burritos

These mini-burritos can be ready in a flash when unexpected company arrives!

15-ounce can black beans, undrained
Nonstick cooking spray
1/2 cup thinly sliced green onions
1/4 teaspoon garlic powder
1/4 teaspoon ground cumin
1/8 teaspoon cayenne pepper
1 teaspoon fresh cilantro
4 6-inch flour tortillas
1/3 cup mild salsa

Place beans in a nonstick skillet coated with cooking spray; mash to desired consistency. Stir in green onions, garlic powder, cumin, cayenne pepper, and cilantro. Cook for 7 minutes over medium heat, until thickened, stirring frequently.

Meanwhile, wrap tortillas in damp paper towels and then in aluminum foil. Bake at 350° for 10 minutes or until softened. Divide bean mixture evenly among tortillas, spreading to within 1/4 inch of edge; roll up jellyroll fashion. Cut each roll into 4 pieces. Serve warm with salsa.

PREPARATION TIME:
10 MINUTES

COOKING TIME:
10 MINUTES

NUTRIENT INFORMATION
(PER SERVING):
SERVINGS PER RECIPE: 16
SERVING SIZE: 1/4 BURRITO
     WITH 1 TEASPOON SALSA

CALORIES	65
PROTEIN	3 G.
CARBOHYDRATE	11 G.
FAT	1 G.
SATURATED FAT	<1 G.
CHOLESTEROL	<1 MG.
SODIUM	79 MG.
DIETARY FIBER	1 G.

% CALORIES FROM:
PROTEIN:	18%
CARBOHYDRATE:	68%
FAT:	14%

FOOD EXCHANGES:
1 STARCH

MAKES 16 SERVINGS.

Italian Bean Dip

PREPARATION TIME:
5 MINUTES

NUTRIENT INFORMATION
(PER SERVING):
SERVINGS PER RECIPE: 20
SERVING SIZE: 1 TABLESPOON
CALORIES   37
PROTEIN   2 G.
CARBOHYDRATE   5 G.
FAT   1 G.
SATURATED FAT   <1 G
CHOLESTEROL   <1 MG.
SODIUM   6 MG.
DIETARY FIBER   1 G.

% CALORIES FROM:
PROTEIN: 22%
CARBOHYDRATE: 54%
FAT: 24%

FOOD EXCHANGES:
1 VEGETABLE

MAKES 1 1/4 CUPS.

A taste of the Mediterranean! Serve this tasty dip with raw vegetables or unsalted crackers.

15 1/2-ounce can Great Northern beans, rinsed and drained
1 tablespoon chopped fresh parsley
1 tablespoon lemon juice
2 teaspoons olive oil
1 teaspoon anchovy paste
1 clove garlic
1/2 teaspoon dried Italian seasoning
1/4 teaspoon Tabasco sauce

Place all ingredients in a blender or food processor. Process until smooth. Spoon mixture into a bowl; stir well.

Magic BEANS

Layered Ranch and Bean Dip

This dip is colorful and easy to prepare. Serve with baked tortilla chips for a fun appetizer!

16-ounce can fat-free refried beans

1 cup fat-free sour cream

1-ounce package dry ranch salad dressing mix

1 cup diced tomatoes

4-ounce can diced green chiles, drained

2 1/4-ounce can sliced black olives, drained

3/4 cup shredded low-fat Monterey Jack cheese

3/4 cup shredded low-fat cheddar cheese

Spread beans on a 10-inch serving platter. Blend sour cream and ranch dressing mix; spread over beans. Layer remaining ingredients over sour cream layer.

PREPARATION TIME:
10 MINUTES

NUTRIENT INFORMATION
(PER SERVING):

SERVINGS PER RECIPE:	10
SERVING SIZE:	1/4 CUP
CALORIES	145
PROTEIN	11 G.
CARBOHYDRATE	14 G.
FAT	5 G.
SATURATED FAT	2 G.
CHOLESTEROL	12 MG.
SODIUM	627 MG.
DIETARY FIBER	2 G.

% CALORIES FROM:

PROTEIN:	30%
CARBOHYDRATE:	39%
FAT:	31%

FOOD EXCHANGES:
1 STARCH
1 MEDIUM-FAT MEAT

MAKES 10 SERVINGS.

Lively Lentil Dip

PREPARATION TIME:
5 MINUTES

COOKING TIME:
40 MINUTES

NUTRIENT INFORMATION
(PER SERVING):
SERVINGS PER RECIPE: 32
SERVING SIZE: 1 TABLESPOON
CALORIES   29
PROTEIN   1 G.
CARBOHYDRATE   4 G.
FAT   1 G.
SATURATED FAT   <1 G.
CHOLESTEROL   0 MG.
SODIUM   26 MG.
DIETARY FIBER   <1 G.

% CALORIES FROM:
PROTEIN: 14%
CARBOHYDRATE: 55%
FAT: 31%

FOOD EXCHANGES:
1 VEGETABLE

MAKES 2 CUPS.

This delicious dip doesn't have a trace of cholesterol!

1 cup lentils, uncooked
2 cups water
1/4 cup fat-free mayonnaise
1/4 cup fat-free sour cream
1 teaspoon dry mustard
1 teaspoon cayenne pepper
1/2 teaspoon paprika

Combine the lentils and water in a saucepan. Bring to a boil. Reduce the heat, cover, and simmer for 40 minutes or until soft. Drain and mash the lentils. Combine with the remaining ingredients, and mix well.

Magic BEANS

Party Time Black-Eyed Pea Dip

Make this appetizer for a crowd at your next fiesta! Refrigerating the prepared dip allows the flavors to blend and the black-eyed peas and hominy to soften. Serve with pita pieces or fat-free crackers.

15-ounce can black-eyed peas, rinsed and drained

15 1/2-ounce can white hominy, rinsed and drained

1 cup chopped red onion

1 cup chopped green pepper

1 tablespoon fresh cilantro or parsley

1 cup mild salsa

4-ounce can chopped green chiles, drained

2 medium tomatoes, chopped and seeded

2 cloves garlic, minced

In a medium bowl, combine all ingredients; mix well. Cover and refrigerate at least 2 hours, stirring occasionally.

PREPARATION TIME:
10 MINUTES

CHILLING TIME:
2 HOURS

NUTRIENT INFORMATION
(PER SERVING):

SERVINGS PER RECIPE:	32
SERVING SIZE:	1/4 CUP
CALORIES	65
PROTEIN	3 G.
CARBOHYDRATE	12 G.
FAT	<1 G.
SATURATED FAT	<1 G.
CHOLESTEROL	0 MG.
SODIUM	187 MG.
DIETARY FIBER	4 G.

% CALORIES FROM:

PROTEIN:	18%
CARBOHYDRATE:	74%
FAT:	8%

FOOD EXCHANGES:
1 STARCH

MAKES 8 CUPS.

Black Bean Dip

PREPARATION TIME:
10 MINUTES

COOKING TIME:
10 MINUTES

NUTRIENT INFORMATION
(PER SERVING):

SERVINGS PER RECIPE: 27
SERVING SIZE: 1 TABLESPOON
CALORIES   37
PROTEIN   2 G.
CARBOHYDRATE   5 G.
FAT   <1 G.
SATURATED FAT   <1 G.
CHOLESTEROL   <1 MG.
SODIUM   32 MG.
DIETARY FIBER   1 G.

% CALORIES FROM:
PROTEIN: 22%
CARBOHYDRATE: 54%
FAT: 24%

FOOD EXCHANGES:
1 VEGETABLE

MAKES 1 2/3 CUPS.

Serve warm or at room temperature with baked tortilla chips.

15-ounce can black beans, rinsed and drained
1 teaspoon olive oil
1/2 cup chopped red onion
2 cloves garlic, minced
1 cup diced tomato
1/2 cup medium picante sauce
1/4 teaspoon ground cumin
1/4 teaspoon chili powder
1/4 cup shredded low-fat Monterey Jack cheese
1/4 cup chopped fresh cilantro
1 tablespoon fresh lime juice

Place beans in a bowl; mash until chunky. Set aside. Heat oil in a medium nonstick skillet over medium heat. Add onion and garlic; sauté 4 minutes or until tender. Add beans, tomato, picante sauce, cumin, and chili powder. Cook 5 minutes or until thickened, stirring constantly. Remove from heat. Add cheese, cilantro, and lime juice, and stir until cheese melts.

Magic BEANS

Cannellini Bean Spread

Puree the potatoes quickly, as they can become sticky if over-processed. Serve this spread on low-fat crackers or baked pita triangles.

1 russet potato (about 1/2 pound), peeled and cut in cubes
2 tablespoons olive oil
2 cups chopped yellow onion
2 cloves garlic, minced
19-ounce can cannellini, rinsed and drained
2 tablespoons chopped fresh oregano
1 teaspoon thyme
1/4 teaspoon black pepper
4 tablespoons plain low-fat yogurt

Place potato cubes in a saucepan. Cover with water, and bring to a boil. Reduce heat, and simmer for about 10 minutes or until potato is tender. Drain well. Heat olive oil in a large skillet over low heat. Add onion and garlic. Cook, stirring for 15 minutes or until vegetables are tender. Add potato, cannellini, oregano, thyme, and black pepper. Cook, stirring often, over very low heat for 5 minutes. Cool slightly. Spoon half of the mixture at a time into a food processor. Add 2 tablespoons of yogurt to each batch. Pulse on and off 8 to 10 times, until slightly smooth. Transfer to a bowl. Cool completely, cover, and refrigerate until ready to use.

PREPARATION TIME:
35 MINUTES

COOLING TIME:
2 HOURS

NUTRIENT INFORMATION
(PER SERVING):
SERVINGS PER RECIPE: 56
SERVING SIZE: 1 TABLESPOON
CALORIES   29
PROTEIN   1 G.
CARBOHYDRATE   4 G.
FAT   1 G.
SATURATED FAT   <1 G.
CHOLESTEROL   <1 MG.
SODIUM   38 MG.
DIETARY FIBER   <1 G.

% CALORIES FROM:
PROTEIN: 14%
CARBOHYDRATE: 55%
FAT: 31%

FOOD EXCHANGES:
1 VEGETABLE

MAKES 3 1/2 CUPS.

Peppery Chick-Pea Dip

PREPARATION TIME:
5 MINUTES

CHILLING TIME:
1 HOUR

NUTRIENT INFORMATION
(PER SERVING):
SERVINGS PER RECIPE: 26
SERVING SIZE: 1 TABLESPOON
CALORIES   29
PROTEIN   1 G.
CARBOHYDRATE   4 G.
FAT   1 G.
SATURATED FAT   <1 G.
CHOLESTEROL   1 MG.
SODIUM   79 MG.
DIETARY FIBER   1 G.

% CALORIES FROM:
PROTEIN: 15%
CARBOHYDRATE: 55%
FAT: 30%

FOOD EXCHANGES:
1 VEGETABLE

MAKES 1 2/3 CUPS.

Chick-peas (alias garbanzo beans) add texture to this full-flavored dip without adding a trace of fat!

15-ounce can garbanzo beans, rinsed and drained
1/2 cup plain nonfat yogurt
1/4 cup nonfat buttermilk salad dressing
2 tablespoons fine dry seasoned bread crumbs
2 teaspoons lemon juice
1/2 teaspoon cayenne pepper
2 tablespoons chopped pitted ripe black olives

In a blender, combine garbanzo beans, yogurt, salad dressing, bread crumbs, lemon juice, and cayenne pepper. Blend until smooth. Stir in olives. Chill, covered, for at least an hour.

Magic BEANS

Black-Eyed Pea Salsa

Canadian bacon gives this salsa a special flavor. Serve with Italian bread or baked tortilla chips; it also makes a tasty topping for baked potatoes or fish fillets.

Nonstick cooking spray

1 cup chopped onion

1/2 cup chopped lean Canadian bacon

2 cloves garlic, minced

1/4 cup chopped green pepper

1/4 teaspoon ground cumin

1/4 teaspoon black pepper

15-ounce can black-eyed peas, rinsed and drained

14 1/2-ounce can no-added-salt tomatoes, undrained and chopped

1/3 cup minced fresh cilantro

1 tablespoon diced green chiles

Coat a large nonstick skillet with cooking spray. Place over medium heat until hot. Add onion, Canadian bacon, garlic, and green pepper; sauté 5 minutes. Stir in cumin, pepper, and black-eyed peas; bring to a boil. Remove from heat. Stir in tomatoes, cilantro, and chiles. Spoon into a bowl. Cover, and chill for at least an hour.

PREPARATION TIME:
10 MINUTES

COOKING TIME:
7 MINUTES

CHILLING TIME:
1 HOUR

NUTRIENT INFORMATION
(PER SERVING):

SERVINGS PER RECIPE:	14
SERVING SIZE:	1/4 CUP
CALORIES	57
PROTEIN	4 G.
CARBOHYDRATE	8 G.
FAT	1 G.
SATURATED FAT	<1 G.
CHOLESTEROL	1 MG.
SODIUM	52 MG.
DIETARY FIBER	3 G.

% CALORIES FROM:

PROTEIN:	28%
CARBOHYDRATE:	56%
FAT:	16%

FOOD EXCHANGES:
1 VEGETABLE

MAKES 3 1/2 CUPS.

Shortcut Guacamole

PREPARATION TIME:
5 MINUTES

NUTRIENT INFORMATION
(PER SERVING):
SERVINGS PER RECIPE: 21
SERVING SIZE: 1 TABLESPOON
CALORIES   28
PROTEIN   2 G.
CARBOHYDRATE   5 G.
FAT   <1 G.
SATURATED FAT   <1 G.
CHOLESTEROL   0 MG.
SODIUM   28 MG.
DIETARY FIBER   1 G.

% CALORIES FROM:
PROTEIN: 28%
CARBOHYDRATE: 71%
FAT: 1%

FOOD EXCHANGES:
1 VEGETABLE

MAKES 1 1/3 CUPS.

Cut the fat by using black beans as the base of this tasty guacamole dip. Using a food processor will trim preparation time.

> 15-ounce can black beans, rinsed and drained
> 1/4 cup chopped onion
> 2 tablespoons lime juice
> 2 tablespoons orange juice
> 2 cloves garlic, minced
> 1/8 teaspoon salt
> 1/4 teaspoon black pepper

Place black beans in a bowl or food processor. Mash or chop until chunky. Add remaining ingredients, and mix thoroughly. Serve with fresh vegetables or baked tortilla chips.

Magic BEANS

Southwest Bean Dip

Red and green bell peppers add color and crunch to this variation of a classic pinto bean dip. Serve with tortilla wedges.

1/2 cup chopped green onions

1 small green bell pepper, chopped

1 small red bell pepper, chopped

1 tablespoon fresh cilantro

16-ounce can pinto beans, rinsed and drained

1 tablespoon cider vinegar

1/2 teaspoon lime juice

1/2 teaspoon olive oil

1/8 teaspoon salt

1/8 teaspoon ground cumin

1/8 teaspoon cayenne pepper

Place green onions, red and green peppers, and cilantro in a food processor. Process until finely chopped. Add remaining ingredients. Pulse until well blended.

PREPARATION TIME:
10 MINUTES

NUTRIENT INFORMATION
(PER SERVING):
SERVINGS PER RECIPE: 24
SERVING SIZE: 1 TABLESPOON
CALORIES 37
PROTEIN 2 G.
CARBOHYDRATE 6 G.
FAT <1 G.
SATURATED FAT <1 G.
CHOLESTEROL 0 MG.
SODIUM 12 MG.
DIETARY FIBER 2 G.

% CALORIES FROM:
PROTEIN: 22%
CARBOHYDRATE: 64%
FAT: 14%

FOOD EXCHANGES:
1 VEGETABLE

MAKES 1 1/2 CUPS.

Spicy Surprise Bean Dip

PREPARATION TIME:
5 MINUTES

COOKING TIME:
4 MINUTES

NUTRIENT INFORMATION
(PER SERVING):
SERVINGS PER RECIPE: 11
SERVING SIZE: 1/4 CUP
CALORIES   93
PROTEIN   4 G.
CARBOHYDRATE   17 G.
FAT   <1 G.
SATURATED FAT   <1 G.
CHOLESTEROL   <1 MG.
SODIUM   214 MG.
DIETARY FIBER   6 G.

% CALORIES FROM:
PROTEIN: 17%
CARBOHYDRATE: 73%
FAT: 10%

FOOD EXCHANGES:
1 STARCH

MAKES 2 3/4 CUPS.

Cereal is the surprise ingredient that gives a nutty taste to this delicious dip!

1 cup All Bran cereal
3/4 cup medium picante sauce
16-ounce can pinto beans, rinsed and drained
1/2 teaspoon ground cumin
1/4 cup chopped red onion
2 tablespoons plain low-fat yogurt
2 tablespoons sliced green onions
2 tablespoons chopped tomato

Measure All Bran, picante sauce, beans, cumin, and red onion into a food processor. Process on low until mixture is smooth. Place mixture in a microwave-safe 1-quart bowl. Cover loosely, and microwave on high 3 to 4 minutes or until thoroughly heated, stirring twice during heating. Pour into a serving dish; dollop with yogurt. Sprinkle onions and tomato over yogurt.

Magic BEANS

Zippy Bean Dip With Crispy Tortilla Chips

This basic bean dip is great with baked tortilla chips!

6 6-inch corn tortillas

Butter-flavored vegetable cooking spray

1/4 teaspoon garlic powder

16-ounce can pinto beans, rinsed and drained

3 tablespoons water

1 tablespoon finely chopped onion

1 tablespoon diced green chiles

1/2 teaspoon ground cumin

1 teaspoon fresh cilantro

1/2 teaspoon white wine vinegar

Coat tortillas with cooking spray; sprinkle with garlic powder. Cut each tortilla into 8 wedges, then place on an ungreased baking sheet. Bake at 350° for 6 minutes. Turn chips; bake an additional 2 to 3 minutes or until golden and crisp. Let cool.

Combine pinto beans, water, onion, green chiles, cumin, cilantro, and vinegar in a small saucepan. Mash beans slightly. Cook over low heat 8 to 10 minutes or until thoroughly heated. Serve warm with tortilla wedges.

PREPARATION TIME:
10 MINUTES

COOKING TIME:
20 MINUTES

NUTRIENT INFORMATION
(PER SERVING):

SERVINGS PER RECIPE: 6

SERVING SIZE: 1/8 TORTILLA
WEDGE WITH 2 TABLESPOONS
BEAN DIP

CALORIES	165
PROTEIN	8 G.
CARBOHYDRATE	31 G.
FAT	1 G.
SATURATED FAT	<1 G.
CHOLESTEROL	0 MG.
SODIUM	42 MG.
DIETARY FIBER	6 G.

% CALORIES FROM:

PROTEIN:	19%
CARBOHYDRATE:	75%
FAT:	6%

FOOD EXCHANGES:
2 STARCH

MAKES 6 SERVINGS.

Turkey Taco Bean Dip

PREPARATION TIME:
10 MINUTES

COOKING TIME:
8 MINUTES

NUTRIENT INFORMATION
(PER SERVING):
SERVINGS PER RECIPE: 32
SERVING SIZE: 1 TABLESPOON
CALORIES   33
PROTEIN   3 G.
CARBOHYDRATE   3 G.
FAT   1 G.
SATURATED FAT   <1 G.
CHOLESTEROL   6 MG.
SODIUM   21 MG.
DIETARY FIBER   1 G.

% CALORIES FROM:
PROTEIN: 36%
CARBOHYDRATE: 36%
FAT: 27%

FOOD EXCHANGES:
1 VEGETABLE

MAKES 2 CUPS.

Using the microwave speeds the preparation time of this flavorful and hearty dip. Serve with baked tortilla chips to keep fat content low.

1/2 pound lean ground turkey

1 large tomato, seeded and chopped

1 tablespoon diced green chiles

2 green onions, chopped

1 cup canned pinto beans, rinsed and drained, then mashed

1/4 cup diced green bell pepper

1/4 cup diced red bell pepper

3 tablespoons chopped onions

1 clove garlic, minced

1 1/2 teaspoons chili powder

1/2 teaspoon ground cumin

1/4 teaspoon fresh cilantro

1/4 cup finely shredded lettuce

1/4 cup fat-free shredded cheddar cheese

Crumble the turkey into a 1 1/2-quart casserole. Microwave on high until the meat is mostly brown (2 to 3 minutes). Drain fat. While the meat is cooking, combine the tomato, green chiles, and green onions in a blender or food processor. Process until smooth. Add to the meat. Stir in the beans, peppers, onion, garlic, chili powder, cumin, and cilantro. Cover the casserole with a lid, and microwave on high until hot and bubbly, about 5 minutes. Top with lettuce and cheddar cheese.

Magic BEANS

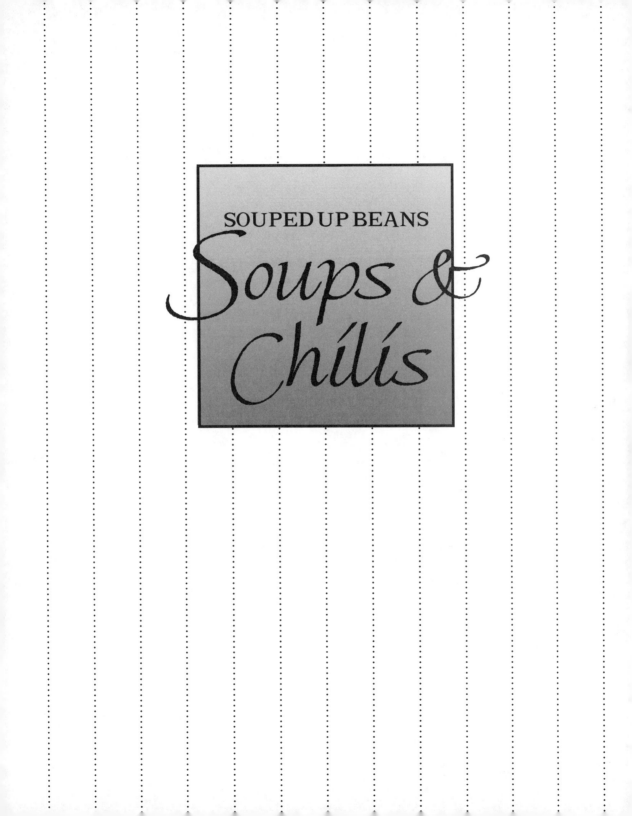

SOUPED UP BEANS

Soups & Chilis

Shortcut Vegetarian Chili

This chili cooks in less than an hour, but tastes like it simmered all day!

Nonstick cooking spray
1 cup chopped onion
2 cloves garlic, minced
1 cup water
1/2 cup diced green bell pepper
2 tablespoons chili powder
1 1/2 teaspoons ground cumin
2 14 1/2-ounce cans no-added-salt stewed tomatoes, undrained
15-ounce can red kidney beans, rinsed and drained
15-ounce can garbanzo beans, rinsed and drained
1/4 cup fat-free sour cream

Coat a large Dutch oven with cooking spray; place over medium heat until hot. Add onion and garlic; sauté 5 minutes. Add next 7 ingredients; bring to a boil. Reduce heat, and simmer, uncovered, 30 minutes. Ladle into individual soup bowls, and top with sour cream.

PREPARATION TIME:	
5 MINUTES	
COOKING TIME:	
40 MINUTES	

NUTRIENT INFORMATION (PER SERVING):

SERVINGS PER RECIPE:	4
SERVING SIZE:	1 1/2 CUPS
CALORIES	328
PROTEIN	15 G.
CARBOHYDRATE	58 G.
FAT	4 G.
SATURATED FAT	<1 G.
CHOLESTEROL	0 MG.
SODIUM	693 MG.
DIETARY FIBER	15 G.

% CALORIES FROM:

PROTEIN:	18%
CARBOHYDRATE:	71%
FAT:	11%

FOOD EXCHANGES:
3 STARCH
3 VEGETABLE
1 FAT

MAKES 4 SERVINGS.

Irene's Zesty Bean and Pasta Stew

PREPARATION TIME:
10 MINUTES

COOKING TIME:
25 MINUTES

NUTRIENT INFORMATION
(PER SERVING):

SERVINGS PER RECIPE: 4
SERVING SIZE: 1 1/2 CUPS
CALORIES   266
PROTEIN   14 G.
CARBOHYDRATE   48 G.
FAT   2 G.
SATURATED FAT   <1 G.
CHOLESTEROL   0 MG.
SODIUM   227 MG.
DIETARY FIBER   9 G.

% CALORIES FROM:
PROTEIN: 21%
CARBOHYDRATE: 72%
FAT: 7%

FOOD EXCHANGES:
3 STARCH
1 VERY LEAN MEAT

MAKES 4 SERVINGS.

This quick-to-fix, hearty soup warms up even the coldest wintry day!

3/4 cup uncooked pasta shells
1/4 cup chopped green bell pepper
1/4 cup chopped red bell pepper
1 teaspoon dried basil
1 teaspoon Worcestershire sauce
1 medium tomato, coarsely chopped
1 medium zucchini, diced
1 small onion, chopped
1 clove garlic, minced
15-ounce can kidney beans, rinsed and drained
1 cup canned navy beans, rinsed and drained
14 1/2-ounce can low-sodium chicken broth

Mix all ingredients in a 2-quart saucepan. Heat to boiling, stirring occasionally; reduce heat. Cover and simmer about 15 minutes, stirring occasionally, until pasta is tender.

Magic BEANS

Pasta e Fagioli

This is a classic Italian bean and pasta soup. Serve with a salad, bread, and fruit for a complete meal.

2 tablespoons olive oil

1 cup chopped onion

2 cloves garlic, minced

2 14 1/2-ounce cans no-added-salt stewed tomatoes, undrained

2 14 1/2-ounce cans low-sodium chicken broth

15 ounce-can cannellini beans, undrained

1/4 cup chopped fresh parsley

1 teaspoon basil leaves

1/4 teaspoon black pepper

1/2 teaspoon oregano

1/2 teaspoon Italian seasoning

1 teaspoon rosemary

4 ounces uncooked small shell pasta

Heat oil in a large Dutch oven over medium heat until hot; add onion and garlic. Cook and stir 5 minutes or until onion is tender. Stir in tomatoes with liquid, chicken broth, beans with liquid, parsley, basil, pepper, oregano, Italian seasoning, and rosemary. Bring to a boil over high heat, stirring occasionally. Reduce heat to low. Simmer, covered, 10 minutes. Add pasta to Dutch oven. Simmer, covered, 10 to 12 minutes or until pasta is just tender. Serve immediately.

PREPARATION TIME:
10 MINUTES

COOKING TIME:
30 MINUTES

NUTRIENT INFORMATION
(PER SERVING):

SERVINGS PER RECIPE:	8
SERVING SIZE:	1 1/2 CUPS
CALORIES	221
PROTEIN	9 G.
CARBOHYDRATE	35 G.
FAT	5 G.
SATURATED FAT	1 G.
CHOLESTEROL	0 MG.
SODIUM	297 MG.
DIETARY FIBER	4 G.

% CALORIES FROM:

PROTEIN:	16%
CARBOHYDRATE:	63%
FAT:	20%

FOOD EXCHANGES:

2 STARCH

2 VEGETABLE

1 FAT

MAKES 8 SERVINGS.

Tipsy Chicken Chili

PREPARATION TIME:
20 MINUTES

COOKING TIME:
75 MINUTES

NUTRIENT INFORMATION
(PER SERVING):

SERVINGS PER RECIPE:	12
SERVING SIZE:	1 CUP
CALORIES	258
PROTEIN	24 G.
CARBOHYDRATE	27 G.
FAT	5 G.
SATURATED FAT	1 G.
CHOLESTEROL	48 MG.
SODIUM	425 MG.
DIETARY FIBER	7 G.

% CALORIES FROM:

PROTEIN:	37%
CARBOHYDRATE:	42%
FAT:	17%
ALCOHOL:	3%

FOOD EXCHANGES:
1 STARCH
2 LEAN MEAT
2 VEGETABLE

MAKES 12 SERVINGS.

Beer is the secret ingredient in this hearty chili. Garbanzo beans add texture and provide extra protein without extra fat.

Nonstick cooking spray

2 teaspoons canola oil

3 cups coarsely chopped onion

1 1/2 cups chopped green bell pepper

1 cup chopped red bell pepper

2 cloves garlic, minced

1 1/2 pounds boneless, skinless chicken breast, cut into 1/2-inch pieces

1/4 cup chili powder

1 tablespoon ground cumin

2 teaspoons ground coriander

1/2 teaspoon salt

1/2 teaspoon cayenne pepper

2 14 1/2-ounce cans no-added-salt whole tomatoes, undrained and chopped

12-ounce can beer

10 1/2-ounce can low-sodium chicken broth

6-ounce can no-added-salt tomato paste

1 bay leaf

2 15-ounce cans garbanzo beans, rinsed and drained

Coat a large Dutch oven with cooking spray; add oil. Place over medium-high heat until hot. Add onions, peppers, and garlic; sauté 5 minutes or until tender. Add chicken, and cook 5 minutes or until browned, stirring constantly. Add chili powder, cumin, coriander, salt, and pepper; cook 1 minute, stirring constantly. Add chopped tomatoes, beer, chicken broth, tomato paste, and bay leaf; bring to a boil. Cover, reduce heat, and simmer 40 minutes, stirring occasionally. Add beans, and cook, uncovered, an additional 20 minutes, stirring occasionally. Discard bay leaf before serving.

Magic BEANS

Peanutty Bean Soup

This recipe uses many foods native to African cuisine, including sweet potatoes and peanuts. It makes a hearty main dish!

1 tablespoon canola oil

1 cup chopped onion

1 medium sweet potato, peeled and diced

1 clove garlic, minced

3 14 1/2-ounce cans low-sodium chicken broth

1 teaspoon thyme

1 teaspoon rosemary

1/2 teaspoon ground cumin

1 cup uncooked brown rice

3 cups thick and chunky salsa

3 16-ounce cans garbanzo beans, rinsed and drained

1 cup zucchini, unpeeled and diced

2/3 cup creamy natural peanut butter

In a large saucepan, heat canola oil over medium-high heat. Sauté onion, sweet potato, and garlic until tender. Add chicken broth, thyme, rosemary, cumin, and rice. Bring to a boil; reduce heat and simmer, covered, until rice is cooked and vegetables are tender, 18 to 20 minutes. Add salsa, beans and zucchini. Cook an additional 10 minutes, until zucchini is tender. Add peanut butter, and stir until melted.

PREPARATION TIME:
10 MINUTES

COOKING TIME:
40 MINUTES

NUTRIENT INFORMATION
(PER SERVING):

SERVINGS PER RECIPE:	10
SERVING SIZE:	1 CUP
CALORIES	368
PROTEIN	15 G.
CARBOHYDRATE	50 G.
FAT	12 G.
SATURATED FAT	2 G.
CHOLESTEROL	54 MG.
SODIUM	864 MG.
DIETARY FIBER	11 G.

% CALORIES FROM:

PROTEIN:	16%
CARBOHYDRATE:	54%
FAT:	29%

FOOD EXCHANGES:
3 STARCH
1 MEDIUM-FAT MEAT
1 VEGETABLE
1 FAT

MAKES 10 SERVINGS.

Simple White Bean Soup

PREPARATION TIME:
10 MINUTES

COOKING TIME:
30 MINUTES

NUTRIENT INFORMATION
(PER SERVING):

SERVINGS PER RECIPE:	4
SERVING SIZE:	1 CUP
CALORIES	381
PROTEIN	25 G.
CARBOHYDRATE	59 G.
FAT	5 G.
SATURATED FAT	1 G.
CHOLESTEROL	2 MG.
SODIUM	397 MG.
DIETARY FIBER	13 G.

% CALORIES FROM:

PROTEIN:	26%
CARBOHYDRATE:	62%
FAT:	12%

FOOD EXCHANGES:
3 STARCH
1 MEDIUM-FAT MEAT
3 VEGETABLE

MAKES 4 SERVINGS.

"Of soup and love, the first is best."—Spanish proverb

1 tablespoon olive oil
1 1/2 cups chopped onion
2 cloves garlic, minced
14 1/2-ounce can low-sodium chicken broth
2 15-ounce cans Great Northern beans, rinsed and drained
1/2 teaspoon salt
1/2 teaspoon Italian seasoning
1/2 teaspoon basil
1/4 teaspoon black pepper
1 cup undiluted evaporated skimmed milk
1 tablespoon chopped fresh parsley

Heat oil in a large, heavy saucepan. Sauté onion and garlic until onion is tender. Add chicken broth, beans, salt, Italian seasoning, basil, and pepper. Bring to a boil. Simmer over low heat for 10 minutes. Pour soup into blender; puree until smooth. Return to saucepan. Slowly stir in evaporated milk. Heat through. Top with fresh parsley.

Magic BEANS

Crockpot Vegetable Chili

This chili is delicious topped with low-fat sour cream!

1 medium zucchini, cut into 1/2-inch slices

1 medium green pepper, coarsely chopped

1/2 cup coarsely chopped onion

1/2 cup coarsely chopped celery

2 cloves garlic, minced

1 tablespoon chili powder

1 teaspoon oregano

1 teaspoon cilantro

1/2 teaspoon ground cumin

2 14 1/2-ounce cans no-added-salt stewed tomatoes, undrained

17-ounce can whole kernel corn, undrained

15-ounce can black beans, rinsed and drained

1 cup chunky salsa

Combine zucchini, green pepper, onion, celery, garlic, chili powder, oregano, cilantro, and cumin in a Crockpot. Stir in stewed tomatoes, corn, black beans, and salsa. Cover and cook on low heat for 8 to 10 hours (or on high for 4 to 5 hours).

PREPARATION TIME:
15 MINUTES

COOKING TIME:
4 TO 10 HOURS

NUTRIENT INFORMATION
(PER SERVING):

SERVINGS PER RECIPE:	4
SERVING SIZE:	1 1/2 CUPS
CALORIES	408
PROTEIN	17 G.
CARBOHYDRATE	76 G.
FAT	4 G.
SATURATED FAT	<1 G.
CHOLESTEROL	0 MG.
SODIUM	623 MG.
DIETARY FIBER	15 G.

% CALORIES FROM:

PROTEIN:	17%
CARBOHYDRATE:	75%
FAT:	8%

FOOD EXCHANGES:
4 STARCH
4 VEGETABLE
1 FAT

MAKES 4 SERVINGS.

Firehouse Lentil Soup

PREPARATION TIME:
10 MINUTES

COOKING TIME:
35 MINUTES

NUTRIENT INFORMATION
(PER SERVING):

SERVINGS PER RECIPE:	6
SERVING SIZE:	1 CUP
CALORIES	118
PROTEIN	5 G.
CARBOHYDRATE	20 G.
FAT	2 G.
SATURATED FAT	<1 G.
CHOLESTEROL	0 MG.
SODIUM	103 MG.
DIETARY FIBER	2 G.

% CALORIES FROM:

PROTEIN:	17%
CARBOHYDRATE:	68%
FAT:	15%

FOOD EXCHANGES:
1 STARCH
1 VEGETABLE

MAKES 6 SERVINGS.

Lentils are a delicious source of low-fat protein; this soup is a spicy way to enjoy their significant health benefits.

1 1/2 cups lentils, uncooked
6 cups water
1/2 teaspoon black pepper
1/2 teaspoon ground cumin
1/2 teaspoon oregano
2 bay leaves
4-ounce can diced green chiles, undrained
1 medium red bell pepper, chopped
1 medium green bell pepper, chopped
1 medium carrot, diced
1/4 cup lime juice
1 tablespoon olive oil

Place first 6 ingredients in a large Dutch oven. Bring to a boil, cover, and simmer until lentils are tender, approximately 20 minutes. Remove 1 cup of lentils, and puree with green chiles in the blender. Add back to the soup. Add the bell peppers and carrots to the soup, and cook until the vegetables are tender, but not overcooked, approximately 15 minutes. Just before serving, discard bay leaves, and stir in lime juice and olive oil.

Magic BEANS

Crowd-Pleasing Chunky Minestrone

This vegetable soup has an Italian accent. The delicate flavor of cannellini beans highlights the spices in this classic soup.

2 teaspoons olive oil

1 1/2 cups chopped onion

1 medium carrot, sliced

1 clove garlic, minced

1/2 cup brown rice, uncooked

1/2 teaspoon Italian seasoning

1/2 teaspoon oregano

1/2 teaspoon basil

2 1/2 cups water

14 1/2-ounce can no-added-salt whole tomatoes, undrained and chopped

10 1/2-ounce can low-sodium chicken broth

1 medium zucchini, halved and sliced thin

1/4 teaspoon salt

1/4 teaspoon pepper

15 1/2-ounce can cannellini beans, rinsed and drained

10-ounce package frozen chopped spinach, thawed and drained

2/3 cup grated Parmesan cheese

Heat oil in a large Dutch oven over medium-high heat. Add onion, carrot, and garlic; sauté 3 minutes. Add next 7 ingredients; bring to a boil. Cover, reduce heat, and simmer 20 minutes. Add zucchini and next 4 ingredients; cook an additional 5 minutes. Ladle into individual soup bowls, and sprinkle with cheese.

PREPARATION TIME:
10 MINUTES

COOKING TIME:
35 MINUTES

NUTRIENT INFORMATION
(PER SERVING):

SERVINGS PER RECIPE:	7
SERVING SIZE:	1 1/2 CUPS
CALORIES	261
PROTEIN	14 G.
CARBOHYDRATE	40 G.
FAT	5 G.
SATURATED FAT	2 G.
CHOLESTEROL	7 MG.
SODIUM	330 MG.
DIETARY FIBER	6 G.

% CALORIES FROM:

PROTEIN:	21%
CARBOHYDRATE:	61%
FAT:	17%

FOOD EXCHANGES:
2 STARCH
1 MEDIUM-FAT MEAT
2 VEGETABLE

MAKES 7 SERVINGS.

Taco Bean Stew

PREPARATION TIME:
10 MINUTES

COOKING TIME:
35 MINUTES

NUTRIENT INFORMATION
(PER SERVING):

SERVINGS PER RECIPE:	8
SERVING SIZE:	1 CUP PLUS
	TOPPINGS
CALORIES	224
PROTEIN	26 G.
CARBOHYDRATE	21 G.
FAT	4 G.
SATURATED FAT	1 G.
CHOLESTEROL	51 MG.
SODIUM	353 MG.
DIETARY FIBER	4 G.

% CALORIES FROM:

PROTEIN:	46%
CARBOHYDRATE:	38%
FAT:	16%

FOOD EXCHANGES:
1 STARCH
3 VERY LEAN MEAT
1 VEGETABLE

MAKES 8 SERVINGS.

This spicy southwestern soup makes a complete meal when served with crusty bread and a fruit salad.

1 pound boneless, skinless chicken breast, cut into bite-sized pieces

15-ounce can kidney beans, rinsed and drained

2 14 1/2-ounce cans no-added-salt whole tomatoes, undrained and chopped

2 13 3/4-ounce cans low-sodium chicken broth

4-ounce can diced green chiles

1/4 teaspoon salt

1/2 teaspoon chili powder

1/4 teaspoon ground cumin

4 corn tortillas, halved

1/2 cup chopped green onions

1/2 cup low-fat shredded Monterey Jack cheese

1/4 cup chopped fresh cilantro

1/4 cup medium taco sauce

Combine first 8 ingredients in a large saucepan. Stir to blend. Bring to a boil. Reduce heat and simmer, uncovered, 30 minutes. Cut each tortilla half into 1-inch pieces, and place the pieces in 8 soup bowls. To each bowl, add 1 cup soup, and top with 1 tablespoon green onions, 1 tablespoon cheese, 1 1/2 teaspoons cilantro, and 1 1/2 teaspoons taco sauce.

Magic BEANS

Black Bean Gazpacho

This cool soup has a spicy touch. Allow plenty of time for the soup to chill while the flavors blend.

2 large tomatoes, seeded and chopped

1 large red bell pepper, chopped

1 large green bell pepper, chopped

1 medium cucumber, peeled and chopped

1 medium stalk celery, thinly sliced

1/4 cup sliced green onions

2 cups no-added-salt tomato juice

1 tablespoon lime juice

2 tablespoons red wine vinegar

1 teaspoon Tabasco sauce

1/4 teaspoon black pepper

1/4 teaspoon Worcestershire sauce

1 clove garlic, minced

15-ounce can black beans, rinsed and drained

1/4 cup fat-free sour cream

Mix all ingredients except sour cream in a large bowl. Cover and refrigerate 6 hours stirring occasionally. Serve with a tablespoon of sour cream.

PREPARATION TIME:
15 MINUTES

CHILLING TIME:
6 HOURS

NUTRIENT INFORMATION
(PER SERVING):

SERVINGS PER RECIPE:	4
SERVING SIZE:	1 1/2 CUPS
CALORIES	225
PROTEIN	12 G.
CARBOHYDRATE	42 G.
FAT	1 G.
SATURATED FAT	<1 G.
CHOLESTEROL	0 MG.
SODIUM	44 MG.
DIETARY FIBER	8 G.

% CALORIES FROM:

PROTEIN:	21%
CARBOHYDRATE:	75%
FAT:	4%

FOOD EXCHANGES:
2 STARCH
2 VEGETABLE

MAKES 4 SERVINGS.

Basic Beef and Vegetable Chili

PREPARATION TIME:
15 MINUTES

COOKING TIME:
2 HOURS

NUTRIENT INFORMATION
(PER SERVING):
SERVINGS PER RECIPE: 8
SERVING SIZE: 1 1/2 CUPS
CALORIES   309
PROTEIN   19 G.
CARBOHYDRATE   38 G.
FAT   9 G.
SATURATED FAT   3 G.
CHOLESTEROL   28 MG.
SODIUM   242 MG.
DIETARY FIBER   10 G.

% CALORIES FROM:
PROTEIN: 25%
CARBOHYDRATE: 49%
FAT: 26%

FOOD EXCHANGES:
2 STARCH
1 MEDIUM-FAT MEAT
2 VEGETABLE
1 FAT

MAKES 8 SERVINGS.

"Next to jazz music, there is nothing that lifts the spirit and strengthens the soul more than a good bowl of chili."
—Harry James

3/4 pound extra lean ground beef

2 cups sliced mushrooms

1/2 cup chopped green bell pepper

1/2 cup chopped red bell pepper

1 cup chopped onion

2 cloves garlic, minced

2 cups diced zucchini

1 1/2 cups water

3 medium carrots, diced

2 tablespoons chili powder

1 tablespoon sugar

2 1/2 teaspoons ground cumin

1 1/2 teaspoons oregano

1/2 teaspoon salt

1/4 teaspoon pepper

1/4 teaspoon Tabasco sauce

2 16-ounce cans kidney beans, rinsed and drained

2 14 1/2-ounce cans no-added-salt whole tomatoes, undrained and chopped

2 8-ounce cans no-added-salt tomato sauce

Cook the beef, mushrooms, bell peppers, onion, and garlic in a large Dutch oven over medium-high heat until browned, stirring to crumble. Drain fat, and return to pan. Add remaining ingredients, and bring to a boil. Partially cover, reduce heat, and simmer 1 1/2 hours or until thickened, stirring occasionally.

Magic BEANS

Red Beans and Rainbows Soup

Multi-colored pasta and red and green peppers make this an eye-catching soup.

15-ounce can red beans, rinsed and drained

8 ounces uncooked multicolored spiral pasta

2 15-ounce cans low-sodium chicken broth

2 tablespoons chopped fresh parsley

1/2 teaspoon ground cumin

1 tablespoon chili powder

1 clove garlic, minced

1/2 large green pepper, cut into very thin strips

1/2 large red pepper, cut into very thin strips

4 green onions, thinly sliced

Place beans in a large saucepan with a tight fitting lid. Add spiral pasta, chicken broth, parsley, cumin, chili powder, garlic, and peppers. Bring the mixture to a boil. Cover pot, and reduce heat to simmer for 15 minutes. Serve in bowls with green onion as a garnish.

PREPARATION TIME:
10 MINUTES

COOKING TIME:
20 MINUTES

NUTRIENT INFORMATION
(PER SERVING):

SERVINGS PER RECIPE:	6
SERVING SIZE:	1 CUP
CALORIES	330
PROTEIN	16 G.
CARBOHYDRATE	62 G.
FAT	2 G.
SATURATED FAT	<1 G.
CHOLESTEROL	0 MG.
SODIUM	105 MG.
DIETARY FIBER	8 G.

% CALORIES FROM:

PROTEIN:	19%
CARBOHYDRATE:	75%
FAT:	6%

FOOD EXCHANGES:
4 STARCH
1 MEDIUM-FAT MEAT

MAKES 6 SERVINGS.

Fruit and Nut Chili

PREPARATION TIME:
20 MINUTES

COOKING TIME:
45 MINUTES

NUTRIENT INFORMATION
(PER SERVING):

SERVINGS PER RECIPE:	8
SERVING SIZE:	1 CUP
CALORIES	398
PROTEIN	18 G.
CARBOHYDRATE	59 G.
FAT	10 G.
SATURATED FAT	1 G.
CHOLESTEROL	5 MG.
SODIUM	342 MG.
DIETARY FIBER	13 G.

% CALORIES FROM:

PROTEIN:	18%
CARBOHYDRATE:	59%
FAT:	23%

FOOD EXCHANGES:
3 STARCH
1 MEDIUM-FAT MEAT
1 VEGETABLE
1 FRUIT
1 FAT

MAKES 8 SERVINGS.

An unusual chili, adapted from a prize-winning recipe, with surprising ingredients and a unique taste. Make it when you feel like serving something different and delicious!

Nonstick cooking spray
1 cup chopped onion
1 clove garlic, minced
2 16-ounce cans no-added-salt tomatoes, undrained and chopped
15-ounce can no-added-salt tomato sauce
14 1/2-ounce can low-sodium chicken broth
2 green bell peppers, chopped
2 4-ounce cans diced green chiles, drained
2 Granny Smith apples, cored and chopped
1 tablespoon chili powder
2 tablespoons unsweetened cocoa powder
1 teaspoon cinnamon
2 15-ounce cans red kidney beans, rinsed and drained
1/2 cup slivered almonds
1/2 cup seedless raisins
1/2 cup low-fat shredded cheddar cheese
1/2 cup fat-free sour cream

Coat a large Dutch oven with cooking spray. Cook onion and garlic until tender. Stir in tomatoes with liquid, tomato sauce, chicken broth, peppers, green chiles, apples, chili powder, cocoa, and cinnamon. Bring to a boil; reduce heat. Cover and simmer for 30 minutes, stirring occasionally. Add kidney beans and almonds. Cook uncovered for an additional 10 minutes. To serve, ladle chili into bowls, and top with raisins, cheddar cheese, and sour cream.

Magic BEANS

Souperior Black Bean Soup

Black bean soup is a traditional dish in South and Central America and the Caribbean. This variation on a classic dish keeps the fat content low and the flavor content high! Top with fat-free sour cream, if desired.

1 tablespoon olive oil

1 cup chopped onion

1 clove garlic, minced

1 medium green bell pepper, chopped

2 15-ounce cans black beans, rinsed and drained

14 1/2-ounce can no-added-salt stewed tomatoes, undrained and chopped

10 1/2-ounce can low-sodium chicken broth

1/2 cup picante sauce

1/4 cup water

1 teaspoon ground cumin

2 tablespoons fresh lime juice

1 tablespoon cilantro

Heat oil in a large nonstick saucepan over medium heat until hot. Add onion, garlic, and green pepper; sauté until tender. Add remaining ingredients, except lime juice and cilantro; stir well. Bring to a boil; reduce heat and simmer, uncovered, 15 minutes. Remove from heat; stir in lime juice. Ladle soup into bowls; garnish with cilantro.

PREPARATION TIME:
10 MINUTES

COOKING TIME:
25 MINUTES

NUTRIENT INFORMATION
(PER SERVING):

SERVINGS PER RECIPE:	6
SERVING SIZE:	1 CUP
CALORIES	251
PROTEIN	14 G.
CARBOHYDRATE	42 G.
FAT	3 G.
SATURATED FAT	1 G.
CHOLESTEROL	1 MG.
SODIUM	158 MG.
DIETARY FIBER	7 G.

% CALORIES FROM:

PROTEIN:	22%
CARBOHYDRATE:	67%
FAT:	11%

FOOD EXCHANGES:
2 STARCH
3 VEGETABLE

MAKES 6 SERVINGS.

Anne's Lemony Lentil Soup

PREPARATION TIME
5 MINUTES

COOKING TIME:
70 MINUTES

NUTRIENT INFORMATION
(PER SERVING):

SERVINGS PER RECIPE:	4
SERVING SIZE:	1 CUP
CALORIES	247
PROTEIN	11 G.
CARBOHYDRATE	35 G.
FAT	7 G.
SATURATED FAT	1 G.
CHOLESTEROL	0 MG.
SODIUM	362 MG.
DIETARY FIBER	6 G.

% CALORIES FROM:

PROTEIN:	18%
CARBOHYDRATE:	57%
FAT:	26%

FOOD EXCHANGES:
2 STARCH
1 MEDIUM-FAT MEAT
1 VEGETABLE

MAKES 4 SERVINGS.

The tart taste of lemon brightens up this protein-packed lentil soup.

2 tablespoons olive oil

2 medium onions, chopped

1 clove garlic, minced

1/2 teaspoon rosemary

1 1/4 cups lentils, uncooked

3 cups water

1/2 teaspoon salt

10-ounce package frozen chopped spinach, thawed and drained

1 teaspoon grated lemon peel

2 teaspoons lemon juice

Heat oil in a large saucepan over medium heat. Cook onions, garlic, and rosemary in oil until onions are tender. Stir in lentils, water, and salt. Heat to boiling; reduce heat. Cover and simmer 1 hour. Stir in spinach, lemon peel, and lemon juice. Cover and simmer about 5 minutes, or until spinach is tender.

Magic BEANS

New Orleans Shrimp Soup

"Red beans and ricely yours" is the way Louis Armstrong signed his letters. Shrimp makes a delicious addition to this New Orleans classic.

1 tablespoon canola oil

1 cup chopped onion

1/2 cup coarsely chopped celery

1 clove garlic, minced

1/2 cup chopped green bell pepper

1/2 cup chopped red bell pepper

2 tablespoons flour

1 1/2 cups water

1/4 cup brown rice, uncooked

1 teaspoon chili powder

1/2 teaspoon ground cumin

1/4 teaspoon salt

14 1/2-ounce can no-added-salt whole tomatoes, undrained and chopped

10 1/2-ounce can low-sodium chicken broth

3/4 pound small fresh unpeeled shrimp

15 1/2-ounce can red beans, rinsed and drained

1 tablespoon lime juice

Heat oil in a large Dutch oven over medium heat. Add onion, celery, garlic, and peppers; sauté 5 minutes. Sprinkle with flour; stir well, and cook an additional minute. Add the next 7 ingredients. Bring to a boil; cover, reduce heat, and simmer for 20 minutes. While soup is simmering, peel and devein shrimp. Add shrimp and red beans to rice mixture, and stir well. Cook, uncovered, 5 minutes or until shrimp is done. Remove from heat, and stir in lime juice.

PREPARATION TIME:
15 MINUTES

COOKING TIME:
35 MINUTES

NUTRIENT INFORMATION
(PER SERVING):
SERVINGS PER RECIPE: 5
SERVING SIZE: 1 1/2 CUPS
CALORIES   293
PROTEIN   24 G.
CARBOHYDRATE   38 G.
FAT   5 G.
SATURATED FAT   1 G.
CHOLESTEROL   103 MG.
SODIUM   265 MG.
DIETARY FIBER   6 G.

% CALORIES FROM:
PROTEIN: 33%
CARBOHYDRATE: 51%
FAT: 16%

FOOD EXCHANGES:
2 STARCH
2 VERY LEAN MEAT
1 VEGETABLE

MAKES 5 SERVINGS.

Lamb and Black Bean Chili

PREPARATION TIME:
10 MINUTES

COOKING TIME:
30 MINUTES

NUTRIENT INFORMATION
(PER SERVING):
SERVINGS PER RECIPE: 7
SERVING SIZE: 1 1/2 CUPS
CALORIES   325
PROTEIN   27 G.
CARBOHYDRATE   43 G.
FAT   5 G.
SATURATED FAT   2 G.
CHOLESTEROL   46 MG.
SODIUM   470 MG.
DIETARY FIBER   8 G.

% CALORIES FROM:
PROTEIN: 33%
CARBOHYDRATE: 53%
FAT: 14%

FOOD EXCHANGES:
3 STARCH
3 VERY LEAN MEAT

MAKES 7 SERVINGS.

This quick-cooking chili uses lamb, a lower-fat alternative to ground beef.

Nonstick cooking spray
1 pound lean ground lamb
1/2 cup chopped onion
1/2 cup chopped green bell pepper
1 1/2 tablespoons chili powder
2 teaspoons ground cumin
1 teaspoon paprika
1/4 teaspoon salt
1/2 teaspoon cayenne pepper
3 8-ounce cans no-added-salt tomato sauce
2 15-ounce cans black beans, rinsed and drained
14 1/2-ounce can no-added-salt whole tomatoes, undrained and chopped
13 3/4-ounce can low-sodium chicken broth
2 4-ounce cans diced green chiles, undrained

Coat a large Dutch oven with cooking spray; place over medium-high heat until hot. Add lamb, onion, and green pepper. Cook until browned, stirring to crumble. Drain well; wipe drippings from pan with a paper towel. Return lamb mixture to pan. Add all remaining ingredients, and bring to a boil. Reduce heat and simmer, uncovered, 15 minutes, stirring occasionally.

Magic BEANS

Old-Fashioned Pinto Bean Soup

Many families have an old-fashioned bean soup recipe that's been handed down for generations. This one has been lightened up in fat and sodium. Serve with Black Bean Cornbread!

Nonstick cooking spray

1/2 cup finely chopped green bell pepper

1/2 cup finely chopped red bell pepper

2 15 1/2-ounce cans pinto beans, undrained

14 1/2-ounce can no-added-salt whole tomatoes, undrained and chopped

4-ounce can diced green chiles, drained

1/2 cup water

1 1/2 teaspoons ground cumin

1/4 teaspoon cayenne pepper

1/2 teaspoon basil

3 sliced green onions

Coat a saucepan with cooking spray. Place over medium-high heat until hot. Add bell peppers; sauté 2 minutes. Remove from heat; add 1 can pinto beans, and mash. Add remaining beans, and next 6 ingredients; stir well. Bring to a boil. Reduce heat and simmer uncovered 10 minutes, stirring occasionally. To serve, ladle soup into bowls, and top with green onions.

PREPARATION TIME:
10 MINUTES

COOKING TIME:
20 MINUTES

NUTRIENT INFORMATION
(PER SERVING):

SERVINGS PER RECIPE:	6
SERVING SIZE:	1 CUP
CALORIES	233
PROTEIN	13 G.
CARBOHYDRATE	43 G.
FAT	1 G.
SATURATED FAT	<1 G.
CHOLESTEROL	0 MG.
SODIUM	181 MG.
DIETARY FIBER	12 G.

% CALORIES FROM:

PROTEIN:	22%
CARBOHYDRATE:	73%
FAT:	4%

FOOD EXCHANGES:
3 STARCH
1 VERY LEAN MEAT

MAKES 6 SERVINGS.

Silky Lentil Soup

PREPARATION TIME:
10 MINUTES

COOKING TIME:
65 MINUTES

NUTRIENT INFORMATION
(PER SERVING):
SERVINGS PER RECIPE: 6
SERVING SIZE: 1 1/2 CUPS
CALORIES   209
PROTEIN   10 G.
CARBOHYDRATE   31 G.
FAT   5 G.
SATURATED FAT   1 G.
CHOLESTEROL   6 MG.
SODIUM   296 MG.
DIETARY FIBER   3 G.

% CALORIES FROM:
PROTEIN: 19%
CARBOHYDRATE: 59%
FAT: 22%

FOOD EXCHANGES:
2 STARCH
1 VEGETABLE
1 FAT

MAKES 6 SERVINGS.

Use a food processor or blender to get the smooth, creamy texture needed for this recipe.

Nonstick cooking spray
1 tablespoon canola oil
2 medium carrots, sliced
1 medium onion, chopped
1 medium green pepper, chopped
2 cups water
1 cup lentils, uncooked
1/3 cup brown rice, uncooked
1/2 teaspoon salt
1/2 teaspoon ground cumin
1/2 teaspoon black pepper
2 13 3/4-ounce cans low-sodium chicken broth
8-ounce can no-added-salt tomato sauce
2 cups 2% milk

Coat a large Dutch oven with cooking spray; add oil. Place over medium-high heat until hot. Add carrots, onion, and green pepper; sauté 5 minutes or until tender. Add water and all remaining ingredients except milk; stir well. Bring to a boil; cover, reduce heat, and simmer 45 minutes or until lentils are tender. Put half of the lentil mixture in a blender or food processor. Process until smooth. Pour puree into a bowl. Repeat with remaining lentil mixture. Return all puree to Dutch oven; stir in milk. Cook over low heat for 10 minutes or until thoroughly heated.

Magic BEANS

Economy Hominy and Bean Soup

This soup is low in fat, inexpensive, and quick-to-fix!

2 15-ounce cans Great Northern beans, undrained

15 1/2-ounce can hominy, undrained

14 1/2-ounce can no-added-salt stewed tomatoes

11 1/2-ounce can bean with bacon soup, undiluted

10-ounce can diced tomatoes and green chiles

11-ounce can whole kernel corn

1 1/2 cups water

2 bay leaves

1 cup diced celery

1 tablespoon cilantro

1 teaspoon ground cumin

1 cup shredded low-fat sharp Cheddar cheese

Combine all ingredients except cheese in a large Dutch oven. Bring to a boil; cover, reduce heat, and simmer 30 minutes. Remove bay leaves. Ladle soup into bowls, and sprinkle each serving with 2 tablespoons cheese.

PREPARATION TIME:
10 MINUTES

COOKING TIME:
35 MINUTES

NUTRIENT INFORMATION
(PER SERVING):

SERVINGS PER RECIPE:	10
SERVING SIZE:	1 CUP
CALORIES	269
PROTEIN	14 G.
CARBOHYDRATE	42 G.
FAT	5 G.
SATURATED FAT	2 G.
CHOLESTEROL	9 MG.
SODIUM	634 MG.
DIETARY FIBER	4 G.

% CALORIES FROM:

PROTEIN:	21%
CARBOHYDRATE:	62%
FAT:	17%

FOOD EXCHANGES:
3 STARCH
1 MEDIUM-FAT MEAT

MAKES 10 SERVINGS.

Tami's White Chili

PREPARATION TIME:
15 MINUTES

COOKING TIME:
30 MINUTES

NUTRIENT INFORMATION
(PER SERVING):
SERVINGS PER RECIPE: 6
SERVING SIZE: 1 1/2 CUPS
CALORIES   342
PROTEIN   35 G.
CARBOHYDRATE   37 G.
FAT   6 G.
SATURATED FAT   2 G.
CHOLESTEROL   42 MG.
SODIUM   642 MG.
DIETARY FIBER   1 G.

% CALORIES FROM:
PROTEIN: 41%
CARBOHYDRATE: 43%
FAT: 16%

FOOD EXCHANGES:
2 STARCH
4 VERY LEAN MEAT
1 VEGETABLE

MAKES 6 SERVINGS.

Chicken and chicken broth give this chili a different twist.

2 15-ounce cans navy beans, rinsed and drained
2 14 1/2-ounce cans low-sodium chicken broth
1 cup water
1 1/4 cups chopped onion
1 clove garlic, minced
2 cups chopped cooked chicken
1 teaspoon ground cumin
3/4 teaspoon oregano
1/2 teaspoon cayenne pepper
4-ounce can diced green chiles, drained
3/4 cup shredded low-fat Monterey Jack cheese

Combine all ingredients except cheese in a large pot. Cover and simmer at least 30 minutes. Cook longer for a thicker chili. Spoon into bowls, and sprinkle with cheese.

Magic BEANS

BEANS AND GREENS

Salads

Hoppin' John Salad

This recipe is a salad version of the traditional southern main dish. It uses black-eyed peas, said to bring good luck when served on New Year's Day.

2 16-ounce cans black-eyed peas, rinsed and drained

3 cups cooked white rice

1/4 pound cooked Canadian bacon, finely chopped

1 small red onion, minced

1 rib celery, thinly sliced

2 tablespoons red wine vinegar

1 tablespoon canola oil

1 clove garlic, minced

1 teaspoon hot pepper sauce

1/2 teaspoon salt

Combine black-eyed peas, rice, bacon, onion, and celery in a large bowl. Combine vinegar, oil, garlic, hot sauce, and salt in a small bowl until well blended. Drizzle over pea mixture; toss to coat. Cover; refrigerate 2 hours.

PREPARATION TIME:
15 MINUTES

CHILLING TIME:
2 HOURS

NUTRIENT INFORMATION
(PER SERVING):

SERVINGS PER RECIPE:	6
SERVING SIZE:	1 CUP
CALORIES	305
PROTEIN	17 G.
CARBOHYDRATE	48 G.
FAT	5 G.
SATURATED FAT	1 G.
CHOLESTEROL	7 MG.
SODIUM	397 MG.
DIETARY FIBER	16 G.

% CALORIES FROM:

PROTEIN:	23%
CARBOHYDRATE:	63%
FAT:	14%

FOOD EXCHANGES:
3 STARCH
1 MEDIUM-FAT MEAT

MAKES 6 SERVINGS.

Tex-Mex Chili Bean Salad

PREPARATION TIME:
15 MINUTES

CHILLING TIME:
8 HOURS

NUTRIENT INFORMATION
(PER SERVING):

SERVINGS PER RECIPE: 10
SERVING SIZE: 1 CUP
CALORIES   204
PROTEIN   9 G.
CARBOHYDRATE   33 G.
FAT   4 G.
SATURATED FAT   1 G.
CHOLESTEROL   0 MG.
SODIUM   422 MG.
DIETARY FIBER   7 G.

% CALORIES FROM:
PROTEIN: 18%
CARBOHYDRATE: 65%
FAT: 18%

FOOD EXCHANGES:
2 STARCH
1 VEGETABLE
1 FAT

MAKES 10 SERVINGS.

This makes a great salad, or can be served in pita bread for a main dish sandwich.

16-ounce can kidney beans, rinsed and drained
16-ounce can pinto beans, rinsed and drained
16-ounce can garbanzo beans, rinsed and drained
16-ounce can no-added-salt whole kernel corn, drained
1/2 cup chopped green onions
1/2 cup chopped green bell pepper
1/2 cup chopped red bell pepper
1/4 cup chopped parsley
1 cup sliced celery
4-ounce can diced green chilies, drained

Dressing:
2 tablespoons olive oil
1/4 cup vinegar
1 clove garlic, minced
1 teaspoon chili powder
1/2 teaspoon cilantro
1 teaspoon oregano
1/4 teaspoon ground cumin
1/8 teaspoon Tabasco sauce

Combine all the salad ingredients in a large bowl. Mix all the dressing ingredients together. Pour dressing over salad, mix well, and chill 8 hours or overnight, stirring occasionally.

Magic BEANS

Mediterranean Bean Salad

Feta cheese, the topper in this salad, is Greek in origin but is now being produced in America with cow's milk instead of the traditional sheep or goat milk. It has approximately one-third less fat than most other cheeses.

1 1/3 cups uncooked bow-tie pasta

1 cup canned garbanzo beans, rinsed and drained

1 cup canned artichoke hearts, rinsed, drained, and quartered

3/4 cup sliced and halved zucchini

1/2 medium red pepper, chopped

1/4 cup chopped red onion

Dressing:

3 tablespoons lemon juice

2 tablespoons olive oil

1/2 teaspoon Italian seasoning

1/8 teaspoon black pepper

1/8 teaspoon garlic powder

2 tablespoons crumbled feta cheese

Cook pasta according to package directions, omitting salt. Rinse with cool water; drain. Cool. Combine pasta, beans, artichoke hearts, zucchini, red pepper, and onion in a large bowl.

Combine lemon juice, oil, Italian seasoning, pepper, and garlic powder in a small bowl until well blended. Drizzle over pasta mixture. Toss to coat. Top with cheese before serving.

PREPARATION TIME:
10 MINUTES

COOKING TIME:
8 MINUTES

NUTRIENT INFORMATION
(PER SERVING):

SERVINGS PER RECIPE:	6
SERVING SIZE:	1 CUP
CALORIES	222
PROTEIN	8 G.
CARBOHYDRATE	34 G.
FAT	6 G.
SATURATED FAT	2 G.
CHOLESTEROL	5 MG.
SODIUM	97 MG.
DIETARY FIBER	4 G.

% CALORIES FROM:

PROTEIN:	14%
CARBOHYDRATE:	61%
FAT:	24%

FOOD EXCHANGES:
2 STARCH
1 VEGETABLE
1 FAT

MAKES 6 SERVINGS.

Quick Bean Salad

PREPARATION TIME:
5 MINUTES

CHILLING TIME:
8 HOURS

NUTRIENT INFORMATION
(PER SERVING):

SERVINGS PER RECIPE:	8
SERVING SIZE:	3/4 CUP
CALORIES	101
PROTEIN	5 G.
CARBOHYDRATE	18 G.
FAT	1 G.
SATURATED FAT	<1 G.
CHOLESTEROL	0 MG.
SODIUM	357 MG.
DIETARY FIBER	6 G.

% CALORIES FROM:

PROTEIN:	20%
CARBOHYDRATE:	72%
FAT:	9%

FOOD EXCHANGES:
1 STARCH
1 VEGETABLE

MAKES 8 SERVINGS.

This tastes best when chilled overnight.

16-ounce can garbanzo beans, rinsed and drained

16-ounce can French-style green beans, drained

14-ounce can artichoke hearts, rinsed, drained, and quartered

1/2 cup fat-free Italian salad dressing

Combine first 3 ingredients in a large bowl, tossing lightly. Pour dressing over vegetables, and toss gently. Chill well before serving.

Magic BEANS

Black and White Salad

This salad is colorful, tasty, and easy to prepare!

2 cups cooked rice, cooled to room temperature
1 cup canned black beans, rinsed and drained
1 cup chopped fresh tomato
1/2 cup shredded low-fat cheddar cheese
1 tablespoon chopped fresh parsley
1/2 cup fat-free Italian salad dressing
1 tablespoon fresh lime juice
Lettuce leaves

Combine rice, beans, tomato, cheese, and parsley in a large bowl. Mix salad dressing and lime juice. Pour over rice mixture; toss. Serve on lettuce leaves.

PREPARATION TIME:
5 MINUTES

COOKING TIME:
20 MINUTES

NUTRIENT INFORMATION
(PER SERVING):
SERVINGS PER RECIPE: 4
SERVING SIZE: 1 CUP
CALORIES   242
PROTEIN   15 G.
CARBOHYDRATE   32 G.
FAT   6 G.
SATURATED FAT   3 G.
CHOLESTEROL   20 MG.
SODIUM   443 MG.
DIETARY FIBER   3 G.

% CALORIES FROM:
PROTEIN: 25%
CARBOHYDRATE: 53%
FAT: 22%

FOOD EXCHANGES:
2 STARCH
1 MEDIUM-FAT MEAT

MAKES 4 SERVINGS.

Garbanzo Salad

PREPARATION TIME:
10 MINUTES

CHILLING TIME:
1 HOUR

NUTRIENT INFORMATION
(PER SERVING):

SERVINGS PER RECIPE:	8
SERVING SIZE:	1/2 CUP
CALORIES	103
PROTEIN	4 G.
CARBOHYDRATE	15 G.
FAT	3 G.
SATURATED FAT	<1 G.
CHOLESTEROL	0 MG.
SODIUM	352 MG.
DIETARY FIBER	4 G.

% CALORIES FROM:

PROTEIN:	16%
CARBOHYDRATE:	58%
FAT:	26%

FOOD EXCHANGES:
1 STARCH
1 FAT

MAKES 8 SERVINGS.

The garbanzo bean is one of the most nutritious members of the bean family; it's rich in protein, calcium, iron, and B vitamins. Enjoy this healthy and tasty recipe!

15-ounce can garbanzo beans, rinsed and drained
3/4 cup chopped purple onion
1 medium tomato, peeled, seeded, and chopped
1 cup diced red bell pepper
1/2 cup chopped ripe olives
1 cup celery

Dressing:
3 tablespoons minced fresh parsley
2 tablespoons lemon juice
2 tablespoons red wine vinegar
3 tablespoons canned low-sodium chicken broth
1 teaspoon olive oil
1/4 teaspoon salt
1/4 teaspoon pepper
1 clove garlic, minced

Combine garbanzo beans, onion, tomato, red pepper, olives, and celery in a bowl. Toss well. Combine dressing ingredients in a small bowl; beat well with a wire whisk. Pour dressing over vegetable mixture, and toss gently. Cover and chill 1 hour.

Magic BEANS

Saucy Lentil Salad

Farmers in Washington and Idaho grow approximately 135 million pounds of lentils annually.

1/2 cup lentils, uncooked

1 1/2 cups water

1 cup uncooked brown rice

1/2 cup fat-free Italian salad dressing

1 small tomato, diced

1/4 cup chopped green bell pepper

1/4 cup chopped red bell pepper

1/4 cup chopped onion

2 tablespoons chopped celery

2 tablespoons sliced, pimento-stuffed green olives

Rinse lentils, and cook in water for 20 minutes or until tender; drain. Check lentils for tenderness after 15 minutes of simmering; they should be tender and firm, but not soft. While lentils are simmering, cook brown rice according to package directions. Combine remaining ingredients. Mix with lentils and rice; toss, and chill for 2 hours.

PREPARATION TIME:
10 MINUTES

COOKING TIME:
20 MINUTES

CHILLING TIME:
2 HOURS

NUTRIENT INFORMATION
(PER SERVING):

SERVINGS PER RECIPE:	6
SERVING SIZE:	1/2 CUP
CALORIES	105
PROTEIN	4 G.
CARBOHYDRATE	20 G.
FAT	1 G.
SATURATED FAT	<1 G.
CHOLESTEROL	0 MG.
SODIUM	322 MG.
DIETARY FIBER	2 G.

% CALORIES FROM:

PROTEIN:	15%
CARBOHYDRATE:	76%
FAT:	9%

FOOD EXCHANGES:
1 STARCH
1 VEGETABLE

MAKES 6 SERVINGS.

Make-Ahead Black-Eyed Pea Salad

PREPARATION TIME:
10 MINUTES

COOKING TIME:
50 MINUTES

CHILLING TIME
8 HOURS

NUTRIENT INFORMATION
(PER SERVING):
SERVINGS PER RECIPE: 6
SERVING SIZE: 1/2 CUP
CALORIES   154
PROTEIN   9 G.
CARBOHYDRATE   25 G.
FAT   2 G.
SATURATED FAT   <1 G.
CHOLESTEROL   0 MG.
SODIUM   359 MG.
DIETARY FIBER   10 G.

% CALORIES FROM:
PROTEIN: 23%
CARBOHYDRATE: 65%
FAT: 12%

FOOD EXCHANGES:
1 STARCH
2 VEGETABLE

MAKES 6 SERVINGS.

Make this tangy salad the night before you need it to allow plenty of time for the black-eyed peas to marinate in the dressing.

1 1/2 cups water
1 medium onion, cut in half
1/2 teaspoon salt
1/2 teaspoon cayenne pepper
1/8 teaspoon hickory-flavored liquid smoke
16-ounce package frozen black-eyed peas
1/3 cup rings sliced from a small purple onion
4 cups leaf lettuce

Dressing:
1/2 cup chopped red bell pepper
3 tablespoons chopped fresh parsley
1/2 cup raspberry wine vinegar
1/4 cup water
1 teaspoon olive oil
1/4 teaspoon salt
1/4 teaspoon pepper
1 clove garlic, minced
1/8 teaspoon hot sauce

Combine water, onion, salt, cayenne pepper, and liquid smoke in a medium saucepan; bring to a boil. Add peas and return to a boil. Cover, reduce heat, and simmer 40 to 45 minutes or until peas are tender. Remove and discard onion; drain well. Rinse with cold water, and drain again. Transfer to a medium bowl; set aside. Combine red pepper, parsley, vinegar, water, olive oil, salt, pepper, garlic, and hot sauce. Pour over peas, tossing gently to coat. Cover and refrigerate 8 hours, stirring occasionally. Add purple onion just before serving. Serve over lettuce leaves on individual plates.

Magic BEANS

Four-Bean Salad

This four-bean combination makes a great side dish!

16-ounce can Great Northern beans, rinsed and drained

16-ounce can red kidney beans, rinsed and drained

16-ounce can no-added-salt cut green beans, rinsed and drained

15-ounce can garbanzo beans, rinsed and drained

1 pint cherry tomatoes, halved

1 green bell pepper, cut into 1-inch strips

3/4 cup chopped green onions

1/3 cup sliced ripe olives

Dressing:

1/2 cup red wine vinegar

3 tablespoons olive oil

1 tablespoon water

1 teaspoon sugar

1 teaspoon dry mustard

1/4 teaspoon cilantro

1/8 teaspoon pepper

1 clove garlic, minced

Combine the salad ingredients in a large bowl; set aside. Combine the dressing ingredients in a small bowl, and stir well with a wire whisk. Pour over bean mixture, and stir to blend. Cover and refrigerate for 1 hour.

PREPARATION TIME:
15 MINUTES

CHILLING TIME:
1 HOUR

NUTRIENT INFORMATION
(PER SERVING):

SERVINGS PER RECIPE:	16
SERVING SIZE:	1/2 CUP
CALORIES	136
PROTEIN	6 G.
CARBOHYDRATE	19 G.
FAT	4 G.
SATURATED FAT	1 G.
CHOLESTEROL	0 MG.
SODIUM	135 MG.
DIETARY FIBER	5 G.

% CALORIES FROM:

PROTEIN:	18%
CARBOHYDRATE:	56%
FAT:	26%

FOOD EXCHANGES:
1 STARCH
1 VEGETABLE
1 FAT

MAKES 16 SERVINGS.

Black Bean and Red Cabbage Slaw

PREPARATION TIME:
15 MINUTES

CHILLING TIME:
2 HOURS

NUTRIENT INFORMATION
(PER SERVING):

SERVINGS PER RECIPE:	4
SERVING SIZE:	1 CUP
CALORIES	213
PROTEIN	13 G.
CARBOHYDRATE	38 G.
FAT	1 G.
SATURATED FAT	<1 G.
CHOLESTEROL	1 MG.
SODIUM	354 MG.
DIETARY FIBER	7 G.

% CALORIES FROM:

PROTEIN:	25%
CARBOHYDRATE:	71%
FAT:	4%

FOOD EXCHANGES:
2 STARCH
1 VERY LEAN MEAT
1 VEGETABLE

MAKES 4 SERVINGS.

This tasty recipe is from the Michigan Bean Commission. To vary the color, taste, and texture of this recipe, combine different varieties of cabbage, such as white, Chinese or savoy.

16-ounce can black beans, rinsed and drained
2 1/2 cups finely shredded red cabbage
1/2 cup shredded carrot
1/2 cup chopped purple onion
1/4 cup chopped fresh cilantro

Dressing:
1/2 cup plain low-fat yogurt
1/2 cup salsa
2 tablespoons fat-free mayonnaise
2 teaspoons white wine vinegar
2 teaspoons lime juice

Place salad ingredients in a large bowl. Mix well. Combine dressing ingredients in a separate bowl. Stir well. Pour dressing over bean and vegetable mixture. Mix gently. Cover and chill for at least 2 hours.

Magic BEANS

Veggie-Bean Potluck Salad

Use precut vegetables to put together this dish in a flash!

1/2 cup white vinegar

3 tablespoons olive oil

1 teaspoon oregano

2 cloves garlic, minced

1/4 teaspoon salt

2 cups small cauliflower florets

2 cups small broccoli florets

2 medium carrots, peeled and cut into thin strips

16-ounce can red kidney beans, rinsed and drained

2 cups shredded low-fat mozzarella cheese

In a large bowl, whisk together vinegar, olive oil, oregano, garlic, and salt. Add vegetables, and mix thoroughly. Add cheese; toss lightly. Cover and chill at least 2 hours, stirring occasionally.

PREPARATION TIME:
10 MINUTES

CHILLING TIME:
2 HOURS

NUTRIENT INFORMATION
(PER SERVING):

SERVINGS PER RECIPE:	8
SERVING SIZE:	1 CUP
CALORIES	165
PROTEIN	14 G.
CARBOHYDRATE	16 G.
FAT	5 G.
SATURATED FAT	1 G.
CHOLESTEROL	5 MG.
SODIUM	391 MG.
DIETARY FIBER	4 G.

% CALORIES FROM:

PROTEIN:	34%
CARBOHYDRATE:	39%
FAT:	27%

FOOD EXCHANGES:
1 STARCH
1 VERY LEAN MEAT
1 FAT

MAKES 8 SERVINGS.

Sunshine Black Bean Salad

PREPARATION TIME:
10 MINUTES

NUTRIENT INFORMATION
(PER SERVING):

SERVINGS PER RECIPE:	4
SERVING SIZE:	1 CUP
CALORIES	257
PROTEIN	17 G.
CARBOHYDRATE	36 G.
FAT	5 G.
SATURATED FAT	1 G.
CHOLESTEROL	5 MG.
SODIUM	660 MG.
DIETARY FIBER	6 G.

% CALORIES FROM:

PROTEIN:	26%
CARBOHYDRATE:	56%
FAT:	18%

FOOD EXCHANGES:
2 STARCH
1 MEDIUM-FAT MEAT
1 VEGETABLE

MAKES 4 SERVINGS.

The sweet taste of mandarin oranges provides a nice contrast to the spices in this colorful salad.

11-ounce can mandarin oranges in light syrup, undrained
2 tablespoons red wine vinegar
1 teaspoon olive oil
1 teaspoon Dijon mustard
1/4 teaspoon minced fresh cilantro
1/4 teaspoon ground cumin
1/4 teaspoon pepper
1/2 cup diced low-fat Monterey Jack cheese
1/4 cup chopped red onion
1 clove garlic, minced
15-ounce can black beans, rinsed and drained
1 1/2 cups finely shredded lettuce

Drain oranges, reserving 1 1/2 tablespoons syrup; set oranges aside. Combine the syrup, vinegar, oil, mustard, cilantro, cumin, and pepper; stir with a wire whisk until blended. Add oranges, cheese, onion, garlic, and beans; stir well. Serve on plates lined with lettuce.

Magic BEANS

Fiesta Potato Salad

Try this spicy variation of an old picnic standby!

4 medium potatoes

3 tablespoons canola oil

1/3 cup vinegar

3 teaspoons chili powder

1 teaspoon ground cumin

1/2 teaspoon salt

1 cup canned corn, rinsed and drained

1/2 cup sliced green onion

1 cup sliced celery

1/2 cup chopped green bell pepper

1/2 cup chopped red bell pepper

16-ounce can pinto beans, rinsed and drained

2 1/4-ounce can sliced pitted ripe olives, drained

Peel potatoes, and cut into 1/2-inch cubes. In a 2-quart saucepan, cook potatoes in boiling water until tender, about 10 to 15 minutes; drain. In a large bowl, combine oil, vinegar, chili powder, cumin, and salt. Gently fold in cooked potatoes and remaining ingredients. Cover; refrigerate 2 hours to blend flavors.

PREPARATION TIME:
10 MINUTES

COOKING TIME:
15 MINUTES

CHILLING TIME:
2 HOURS

NUTRIENT INFORMATION
(PER SERVING):

SERVINGS PER RECIPE:	10
SERVING SIZE:	1 CUP
CALORIES	214
PROTEIN	6 G.
CARBOHYDRATE	31 G.
FAT	6 G.
SATURATED FAT	1 G.
CHOLESTEROL	0 MG.
SODIUM	260 MG.
DIETARY FIBER	6 G.

% CALORIES FROM:

PROTEIN:	17%
CARBOHYDRATE:	58%
FAT:	25%

FOOD EXCHANGES:
2 STARCH
1 FAT

MAKES 10 SERVINGS.

Warm Dijon Bean Salad

PREPARATION TIME:
8 MINUTES

COOKING TIME:
3 MINUTES

NUTRIENT INFORMATION
(PER SERVING):

SERVINGS PER RECIPE:	4
SERVING SIZE:	1/2 CUP
CALORIES	95
PROTEIN	5 G.
CARBOHYDRATE	12 G.
FAT	3 G.
SATURATED FAT	<1 G.
CHOLESTEROL	0 MG.
SODIUM	645 MG.
DIETARY FIBER	2 G.

% CALORIES FROM:

PROTEIN:	21%
CARBOHYDRATE:	51%
FAT:	28%

FOOD EXCHANGES:
1 STARCH
1 FAT

MAKES 4 SERVINGS.

This is a nice side salad for seafood.

2 tablespoons white wine vinegar
1 tablespoon Dijon mustard
1 teaspoon canola oil
Nonstick cooking spray
1 1/2 cups frozen cut green beans, thawed and drained
1/2 cup canned red kidney beans, rinsed and drained
1/4 cup thinly sliced celery
1 tablespoon minced purple onion
3 cups Bibb lettuce leaves
2 teaspoons minced red bell pepper
2 teaspoons minced green bell pepper

Combine vinegar, mustard, and canola oil in a bowl; stir well, and set aside. Coat a nonstick skillet with cooking spray; place over medium heat until hot. Add green beans; sauté 2 minutes. Add vinegar mixture, kidney beans, celery, and onion; cook 1 minute, stirring frequently. Spoon onto lettuce leaves; top with bell peppers. Serve warm.

Magic BEANS

Italian Garden Salad

An interesting mix of vegetables complements the rich, full flavor of garbanzo beans in this recipe.

1 tablespoon olive oil

1 small eggplant, peeled and cut into 1-inch cubes

1 large onion, chopped

1 medium potato, peeled and cubed

2 cloves garlic, minced

1/2 cup chopped green bell pepper

1/2 cup chopped red bell pepper

3 tablespoons no-added-salt tomato paste

3 tablespoons red wine vinegar

2 tablespoons capers, drained

1/2 teaspoon Italian seasoning

1/2 teaspoon oregano

1/2 teaspoon basil

2 medium tomatoes, seeded and chopped

16-ounce can garbanzo beans, rinsed and drained

4 slices whole wheat bread, toasted and cut into triangles

2 cups spinach leaves

Heat oil in a medium nonstick skillet over medium-high heat. Cook eggplant, onion, potato, and garlic in oil 8 to 10 minutes, stirring occasionally, until eggplant and potato are crisp-tender. Stir in remaining ingredients except toast and spinach; reduce heat. Cover and simmer 10 minutes. Cover and refrigerate at least 2 hours. Serve over toast and spinach leaves.

PREPARATION TIME:
15 MINUTES

COOKING TIME:
20 MINUTES

CHILLING TIME:
2 HOURS

NUTRIENT INFORMATION
(PER SERVING):

SERVINGS PER RECIPE:	4
SERVING SIZE:	1 1/2 CUPS
CALORIES	384
PROTEIN	14 G.
CARBOHYDRATE	64 G.
FAT	8 G.
SATURATED FAT	1 G.
CHOLESTEROL	4 MG.
SODIUM	560 MG.
DIETARY FIBER	10 G.

% CALORIES FROM:

PROTEIN:	15%
CARBOHYDRATE:	67%
FAT:	19%

FOOD EXCHANGES:
4 STARCH
1 VEGETABLE
1 FAT

MAKES 4 SERVINGS.

Bean and Orzo Salad

PREPARATION TIME:
10 MINUTES

COOKING TIME:
15 MINUTES

NUTRIENT INFORMATION
(PER SERVING):

SERVINGS PER RECIPE: 4
SERVING SIZE: 1 1/2 CUPS
CALORIES   492
PROTEIN   24 G.
CARBOHYDRATE   72 G.
FAT   12 G.
SATURATED FAT   2 G.
CHOLESTEROL   0 MG.
SODIUM   224 MG.
DIETARY FIBER   13 G.

% CALORIES FROM:
PROTEIN: 20%
CARBOHYDRATE: 58%
FAT: 22%

FOOD EXCHANGES:
4 STARCH
1 VERY LEAN MEAT
2 VEGETABLE
2 FAT

MAKES 4 SERVINGS.

This salad is an excellent accompaniment to a meal, yet is as nutritious and satisfying as a main course.

2 15-ounce cans black beans, rinsed and drained
2 1/4-ounce can sliced ripe olives, drained
2 medium tomatoes, seeded and chopped
1/4 cup chopped green onions
1/4 cup chopped fresh cilantro
2 tablespoons olive oil
2 tablespoons lime juice
1/2 teaspoon ground cumin
1/2 teaspoon oregano
1/4 teaspoon pepper
1/8 teaspoon salt
1 1/2 cups cooked rosamarina (orzo) pasta
4 cups chopped fresh spinach

Mix beans, olives, tomatoes, onions, and cilantro in a large bowl. Mix olive oil, lime juice, cumin, oregano, pepper, and salt; toss with bean mixture. Stir in pasta. Serve over spinach.

Magic BEANS

Green Soybean Salad

Fresh green soybeans are popular in Japan and will soon become more readily available in the United States. They can be served warm as a vegetable side dish with a minimum of additional seasoning.

2 cups fresh or frozen green soybeans

4 cups water

1/2 cup finely chopped celery

1/4 cup chopped green bell pepper

1 large tomato, diced

1/2 cup fat-free French dressing

Simmer fresh soybeans for 15 minutes or cook frozen soybeans according to package directions. Drain beans. Combine all ingredients, and toss. Chill 1 hour to serve as a salad.

PREPARATION TIME:
5 MINUTES

COOKING TIME:
15 MINUTES

CHILLING TIME:
1 HOUR

NUTRIENT INFORMATION
(PER SERVING):

SERVINGS PER RECIPE:	4
SERVING SIZE:	1/2 CUP
CALORIES	125
PROTEIN	12 G.
CARBOHYDRATE	18 G.
FAT	<1 G.
SATURATED FAT	<1 G.
CHOLESTEROL	0 MG.
SODIUM	187 MG.
DIETARY FIBER	5 G.

% CALORIES FROM:

PROTEIN:	38%
CARBOHYDRATE:	58%
FAT:	4%

FOOD EXCHANGES:
1 STARCH
1 VERY LEAN MEAT
1 VEGETABLE

MAKES 4 SERVINGS.

Moroccan Lentil Salad

PREPARATION TIME:
15 MINUTES

COOKING TIME:
25 MINUTES

NUTRIENT INFORMATION
(PER SERVING):

SERVINGS PER RECIPE:	4
SERVING SIZE:	1 1/2 CUPS
CALORIES	227
PROTEIN	11 G.
CARBOHYDRATE	30 G.
FAT	7 G.
SATURATED FAT	3 G.
CHOLESTEROL	13 MG.
SODIUM	343 MG.
DIETARY FIBER	4 G.

% CALORIES FROM:

PROTEIN:	19%
CARBOHYDRATE:	53%
FAT:	28%

FOOD EXCHANGES:
2 STARCH
1 VEGETABLE
1 FAT

MAKES 4 SERVINGS.

Enjoy the great taste of lentils in this unusual salad.

1 1/4 cups uncooked lentils
2 1/2 cups water
3 tablespoons lemon juice
1 1/2 tablespoons olive oil
1/2 teaspoon thyme
1/2 teaspoon mint flakes
1/4 teaspoon salt
1/8 teaspoon black pepper
1 clove garlic, minced
1 1/2 cups quartered cherry tomatoes
1 cup diced cucumber
1/2 cup crumbled feta cheese
1/3 cup thinly sliced celery
2 cups romaine lettuce leaves

Place lentils and water in a large saucepan; bring to a boil. Cover, reduce heat, and simmer 20 minutes or until tender. Drain well, and set aside. Combine lemon juice, olive oil, thyme, mint, salt, pepper, and garlic in a medium bowl; stir with a wire whisk until blended. Add lentils, tomatoes, cucumber, cheese, and celery to dressing mixture; toss gently to coat. Serve on plates lined with romaine lettuce.

Magic BEANS

Bean Submarine Salad

This chopped salad is made of many ingredients often found on a submarine sandwich, but the beans and cherries are a surprise!

5 cups chopped cabbage

1 cup canned garbanzo beans, rinsed and drained

1/2 cup diced cooked chicken

1/4 cup diced provolone cheese

1/2 cup diced turkey salami

1/4 cup chopped fresh basil

2 1/2 cups pitted fresh sweet cherries

Dressing:

1 tablespoon balsamic vinegar

1 tablespoon olive oil

1/2 teaspoon sugar

1/8 teaspoon garlic powder

1/8 teaspoon black pepper

Toss cabbage, beans, chicken, cheese, salami, and basil until well mixed. Combine dressing ingredients, and mix well. Pour dressing over cabbage mixture, add cherries, and mix well. Serve on individual salad plates garnished with additional basil leaves.

PREPARATION TIME:
20 MINUTES

NUTRIENT INFORMATION
(PER SERVING):

SERVINGS PER RECIPE:	5
SERVING SIZE:	1 1/2 CUPS
CALORIES	207
PROTEIN	11 G.
CARBOHYDRATE	25 G.
FAT	7 G.
SATURATED FAT	2 G.
CHOLESTEROL	22 MG.
SODIUM	303 MG.
DIETARY FIBER	5 G.

% CALORIES FROM:

PROTEIN:	21%
CARBOHYDRATE:	48%
FAT:	30%

FOOD EXCHANGES:

1 STARCH

1 LEAN MEAT

1 VEGETABLE

1 FAT

MAKES 5 SERVINGS.

Orange Chick-Pea Pasta Salad

PREPARATION TIME:
20 MINUTES

CHILLING TIME:
1 HOUR

NUTRIENT INFORMATION
(PER SERVING):

SERVINGS PER RECIPE: 6
SERVING SIZE: 1 CUP
CALORIES   202
PROTEIN   6 G.
CARBOHYDRATE   31 G.
FAT   6 G.
SATURATED FAT   1 G.
CHOLESTEROL   0 MG.
SODIUM   307 MG.
DIETARY FIBER   7 G.

% CALORIES FROM:
PROTEIN: 12%
CARBOHYDRATE: 61%
FAT: 27%

FOOD EXCHANGES:
2 STARCH
1 FAT

MAKES 6 SERVINGS.

Interesting ingredients make this a super salad!

4 ounces multicolored corkscrew pasta, uncooked

2 navel oranges, peeled, separated into segments, and halved

15-ounce can garbanzo beans, rinsed and drained

3/4 cup broccoli florets

3/4 cup cauliflower florets

2 1/4-ounce can sliced ripe olives, drained

1/2 cup sliced green onion

Dressing:

1/4 cup red wine vinegar

1/4 cup orange juice

1 tablespoon canola oil

1 teaspoon basil

1 teaspoon crushed oregano

1/2 teaspoon rosemary

1 clove garlic, minced

1/4 teaspoon pepper

Cook pasta according to package directions; drain. Rinse with cold water, and drain well again. In a large bowl, combine pasta, orange sections, garbanzo beans, broccoli, cauliflower, olives, and green onion. Combine dressing ingredients in a container with a lid. Cover and shake until blended. Pour dressing mixture over pasta mixture; toss to combine. Cover and chill at least 1 hour, stirring occasionally.

Magic BEANS

South-of-the-Border Black Bean Salad

Jicama, also known as the Mexican potato, is delicately flavored and slightly sweet. It adds a crisp and juicy texture to this savory salad.

Dressing:

1/4 cup red wine vinegar

2 tablespoons olive oil

1/2 teaspoon chili powder

1/4 teaspoon ground cumin

1 small clove garlic, crushed

Salad:

1 cup frozen corn, rinsed to thaw, and drained

1 cup diced jicama

1 medium tomato, seeded and chopped

2 green onions, sliced

2 15-ounce cans black beans, rinsed and drained

Mix all dressing ingredients together in a large bowl. Add salad ingredients. Mix. Chill 2 hours, stirring occasionally.

PREPARATION TIME:
10 MINUTES

CHILLING TIME:
2 HOURS

NUTRIENT INFORMATION
(PER SERVING):

SERVINGS PER RECIPE:	5
SERVING SIZE:	1 CUP
CALORIES	347
PROTEIN	17 G.
CARBOHYDRATE	54 G.
FAT	7 G.
SATURATED FAT	1 G.
CHOLESTEROL	0 MG.
SODIUM	115 MG.
DIETARY FIBER	9 G.

% CALORIES FROM:

PROTEIN:	20%
CARBOHYDRATE:	62%
FAT:	18%

FOOD EXCHANGES:
3 STARCH
2 VEGETABLE
1 VERY LEAN MEAT
1 FAT

MAKES 5 SERVINGS.

Cool Lentil Salad

PREPARATION TIME:
10 MINUTES

COOKING TIME:
25 MINUTES

CHILLING TIME:
8 HOURS

NUTRIENT INFORMATION
(PER SERVING):
SERVINGS PER RECIPE: 4
SERVING SIZE: 1 CUP
CALORIES   237
PROTEIN   10 G.
CARBOHYDRATE   47 G.
FAT   <1 G.
SATURATED FAT   <1 G.
CHOLESTEROL   0 MG.
SODIUM   227 MG.
DIETARY FIBER   6 G.

% CALORIES FROM:
PROTEIN: 17%
CARBOHYDRATE: 79%
FAT: 4%

FOOD EXCHANGES:
3 STARCH
1 VEGETABLE

MAKES 4 SERVINGS.

This lentil salad is a "cool" side dish for your favorite meat or seafood entree. Make it the night before to allow plenty of time for the flavors to meld.

1 cup uncooked lentils

2 cups water

1 cup canned cannellini beans, rinsed and drained

1 cup canned cut green beans, rinsed and drained

1 medium onion, minced

1/2 cup celery, thinly sliced

2 tablespoons chopped red bell pepper

2 tablespoons chopped green bell pepper

Dressing:

1/4 cup vinegar

1/4 cup sugar

1/4 teaspoon sesame seed

1/8 teaspoon salt

1/8 teaspoon black pepper

1 teaspoon low-sodium soy sauce

Place lentils and water in a large saucepan; bring to a boil. Cover, reduce heat, and simmer 20 minutes or until tender. DO NOT DRAIN. Cool slightly. Place lentils, cannellini beans, green beans, onion, celery, and peppers in a bowl. In a separate bowl, combine dressing ingredients. Pour dressing over vegetables. Toss gently, cover, and refrigerate overnight. Serve with a slotted spoon.

Magic BEANS

Barley and Black Bean Salad

This salad combines great taste with a double dose of cholesterol-lowering ingredients—barley and beans. Allow time for the black beans and barley to marinate separately overnight in the savory dressing.

3/4 cup uncooked barley

1/4 cup lime juice

2 tablespoons water

1 tablespoon canola oil

1 teaspoon sugar

1/2 teaspoon garlic powder

1/4 teaspoon salt

1/4 teaspoon black pepper

1/4 teaspoon cayenne pepper

1/4 teaspoon ground cumin

15-ounce can black beans, rinsed and drained

2 cups leaf lettuce

1 medium tomato, chopped

1/4 cup shredded low-fat cheddar cheese

1/4 cup sliced green onions

Cook barley according to package directions. Drain and set aside. Combine lime juice, water, canola oil, sugar, garlic powder, salt, peppers, and cumin in a covered container. Shake well. Pour half of dressing over cooked barley. In a separate container, combine black beans and remaining dressing. Cover and refrigerate barley and beans 8 hours, stirring occasionally. Spoon barley mixture evenly onto 4 lettuce-lined plates. Top with black beans, tomato, cheese, and onions.

PREPARATION TIME:
15 MINUTES

CHILLING TIME:
8 HOURS

NUTRIENT INFORMATION
(PER SERVING):

SERVINGS PER RECIPE:	4
SERVING SIZE:	1/2 CUP
CALORIES	375
PROTEIN	18 G.
CARBOHYDRATE	60 G.
FAT	7 G.
SATURATED FAT	2 G.
CHOLESTEROL	10 MG.
SODIUM	226 MG.
DIETARY FIBER	11 G.

% CALORIES FROM:

PROTEIN:	19%
CARBOHYDRATE:	64%
FAT:	17%

FOOD EXCHANGES:
4 STARCH
1 VERY LEAN MEAT
1 FAT

MAKES 4 SERVINGS.

Simply Delicious White Bean Salad

PREPARATION TIME:
10 MINUTES

NUTRIENT INFORMATION
(PER SERVING):

SERVINGS PER RECIPE:	6
SERVING SIZE:	1/2 CUP
CALORIES	129
PROTEIN	8 G.
CARBOHYDRATE	23 G.
FAT	<1 G.
SATURATED FAT	<1 G.
CHOLESTEROL	0 MG.
SODIUM	94 MG.
DIETARY FIBER	4 G.

% CALORIES FROM:

PROTEIN:	25%
CARBOHYDRATE:	71%
FAT:	4%

FOOD EXCHANGES:
1 STARCH
2 VEGETABLE

MAKES 6 SERVINGS.

This salad practically makes itself—you can put it together in about 10 minutes.

19-ounce can cannellini beans, rinsed and drained
2 medium tomatoes, seeded and chopped
1/3 cup sliced green onions
1/4 cup chopped fresh parsley
1 teaspoon rosemary
3 tablespoons fat-free Dijon vinaigrette salad dressing
3 cups shredded lettuce

Combine beans, tomatoes, onions, parsley, and rosemary in a medium bowl; toss well. Add dressing; mix gently. Serve over shredded lettuce.

Magic BEANS

Greek Pasta Bean Salad

This salad doubles as a side dish or meatless main dish, depending on the size of the servings. Dark red kidney beans add rich flavor and color.

4 cups cooked radiatore (nugget) pasta

2 cups thinly sliced cucumber

1/2 cup chopped red bell pepper

1/2 cup chopped green bell pepper

1/2 cup sliced red onion

1/4 cup Greek olives, pitted and cut in half

1/4 cup finely chopped fresh parsley

3 tablespoons olive oil

1/4 cup lemon juice

1/2 teaspoon oregano

1/4 teaspoon salt

16-ounce can dark red kidney beans, rinsed and drained

2 tablespoons crumbled feta cheese

Mix all ingredients except cheese in a bowl. Cover and refrigerate at least 1 hour to blend flavors. Top with cheese before serving.

PREPARATION TIME:
10 MINUTES

COOKING TIME:
15 MINUTES

CHILLING TIME:
1 HOUR

NUTRIENT INFORMATION
(PER SERVING):

SERVINGS PER RECIPE:	6
SERVING SIZE:	1 1/2 CUPS
CALORIES	314
PROTEIN	11 G.
CARBOHYDRATE	45 G.
FAT	10 G.
SATURATED FAT	2 G.
CHOLESTEROL	5 MG.
SODIUM	194 MG.
DIETARY FIBER	6 G.

% CALORIES FROM:

PROTEIN:	14%
CARBOHYDRATE:	57%
FAT:	29%

FOOD EXCHANGES:
3 STARCH
2 FAT

MAKES 6 SERVINGS.

Festive Lentil Toss

PREPARATION TIME:
15 MINUTES

COOKING TIME:
25 MINUTES

COOLING TIME:
10 MINUTES

NUTRIENT INFORMATION
(PER SERVING):

SERVINGS PER RECIPE:	8
SERVING SIZE:	1 CUP
CALORIES	114
PROTEIN	6 G.
CARBOHYDRATE	18 G.
FAT	2 G.
SATURATED FAT	<1 G.
CHOLESTEROL	0 MG.
SODIUM	84 MG.
DIETARY FIBER	3 G.

% CALORIES FROM:

PROTEIN:	21%
CARBOHYDRATE:	63%
FAT:	16%

FOOD EXCHANGES:
1 STARCH
1 VEGETABLE

MAKES 8 SERVINGS.

This colorful lentil salad is good served "undressed." You may also enjoy it with either fat-free ranch or fat-free Italian salad dressing.

1 cup uncooked lentils
2 cups water
1 head cauliflower, broken into florets
1 bunch broccoli, broken into florets
2 cucumbers, sliced and quartered
1 large carrot, grated
1/2 cup chopped purple onion
8 fresh mushrooms, sliced
1/2 cup sliced olives

Place lentils and water in a large saucepan; bring to a boil. Cover, reduce heat, and simmer 20 minutes or until tender. Drain well, and set aside to cool slightly. Toss lentils with the remaining ingredients, and serve.

Magic BEANS

Black Bean Summer Salad

This salad is great for a summer get-together with friends.

16-ounce can black beans, rinsed and drained

4 ounces low-fat Monterey Jack cheese, cut into
    1/4-inch cubes

8-ounce can whole kernel corn, drained

3/4 cup sliced green onions with tops

3/4 cup thinly sliced celery

1 small red bell pepper, diced

3/4 cup picante sauce

1 tablespoon olive oil

2 tablespoons lemon juice

1 teaspoon ground cumin

1 clove garlic, minced

Combine beans, cheese, corn, onions, celery, and pepper in a large bowl. Combine picante sauce, oil, lemon juice, cumin, and garlic; mix well. Toss with bean mixture. Chill, if desired.

PREPARATION TIME:
15 MINUTES

NUTRIENT INFORMATION
(PER SERVING):

SERVINGS PER RECIPE:	8
SERVING SIZE:	3/4 CUP
CALORIES	182
PROTEIN	10 G.
CARBOHYDRATE	22 G.
FAT	6 G.
SATURATED FAT	2 G.
CHOLESTEROL	10 MG.
SODIUM	314 MG.
DIETARY FIBER	3 G.

% CALORIES FROM:

PROTEIN:	22%
CARBOHYDRATE:	48%
FAT:	30%

FOOD EXCHANGES:
1 STARCH
1 VERY LEAN MEAT
1 VEGETABLE
1 FAT

MAKES 8 SERVINGS.

Oriental Bean Toss

PREPARATION TIME:
15 MINUTES

NUTRIENT INFORMATION
(PER SERVING):

SERVINGS PER RECIPE:	8
SERVING SIZE:	1 1/2 CUPS
CALORIES	188
PROTEIN	9 G.
CARBOHYDRATE	29 G.
FAT	4 G.
SATURATED FAT	<1 G.
CHOLESTEROL	0 MG.
SODIUM	84 MG.
DIETARY FIBER	7 G.

% CALORIES FROM:

PROTEIN:	19%
CARBOHYDRATE:	62%
FAT:	19%

FOOD EXCHANGES:
1 STARCH
3 VEGETABLE
1 FAT

MAKES 8 SERVINGS.

This recipe was adapted from a delectable recipe from the Nebraska Dry Bean Commission.

15-ounce can Great Northern Beans, rinsed and drained
15-ounce can dark red kidney beans, rinsed and drained
4 cups thinly sliced green cabbage
1 cup sliced fresh mushrooms
1 cup bean sprouts
2 tablespoons diced red pepper
8-ounce can sliced water chestnuts, drained

Dressing:
2 tablespoons canola oil
1/4 cup red wine vinegar
1 tablespoon low-sodium soy sauce
1 tablespoon sugar
1/4 teaspoon ginger
1/2 teaspoon garlic powder

Place all salad ingredients in a large salad bowl. Pour dressing ingredients into a covered container, and shake well. Pour prepared dressing over vegetables, and mix well. Serve immediately.

Magic BEANS

Kidney Bean Taco Salad

This taco salad has all the taste, but very little of the fat found in most taco salads.

3 cups canned red kidney beans, rinsed and drained

1/2 cucumber, peeled and chopped

3/4 cup shredded low-fat cheddar cheese

2/3 cup chopped celery

1 medium tomato, diced

1/2 cup sliced black olives

1/2 cup chopped green bell pepper

1 small onion, sliced

1/2 head iceberg lettuce, chopped

1/2 cup fat-free French salad dressing

4 cups baked tortilla chips

Combine all ingredients except tortilla chips in a large bowl. Toss to combine. Crush the chips, sprinkle them on the salad, and serve.

PREPARATION TIME:
15 MINUTES

NUTRIENT INFORMATION
(PER SERVING):

SERVINGS PER RECIPE:	8
SERVING SIZE:	2/3 CUP
CALORIES	289
PROTEIN	12 G.
CARBOHYDRATE	40 G.
FAT	9 G.
SATURATED FAT	2 G.
CHOLESTEROL	7 MG.
SODIUM	418 MG.
DIETARY FIBER	7 G.

% CALORIES FROM:

PROTEIN:	17%
CARBOHYDRATE:	55%
FAT:	28%

FOOD EXCHANGES:
2 STARCH
1 VEGETABLE
2 FAT

MAKES 8 SERVINGS.

Seven-Layer Vegetable Bean Salad

PREPARATION TIME:
15 MINUTES

CHILLING TIME:
8 HOURS

NUTRIENT INFORMATION
(PER SERVING):

SERVINGS PER RECIPE:	8
SERVING SIZE:	1 CUP
CALORIES	227
PROTEIN	13 G.
CARBOHYDRATE	28 G.
FAT	7 G.
SATURATED FAT	3 G.
CHOLESTEROL	15 MG.
SODIUM	733 MG.
DIETARY FIBER	7 G.

% CALORIES FROM:

PROTEIN:	23%
CARBOHYDRATE:	49%
FAT:	28%

FOOD EXCHANGES:
2 STARCH
1 LEAN MEAT
1 FAT

MAKES 8 SERVINGS.

This make-ahead main dish salad is popular at church suppers and potluck dinners. At home, serve with warm bread for a complete meal.

8 cups bite-sized spinach pieces

15-ounce can garbanzo beans, rinsed and drained

8-ounce can sliced water chestnuts, drained

1/2 cup pimento-stuffed olives

1 cup shredded low-fat cheddar cheese

1 small purple onion, thinly sliced and separated
  into rings

10-ounce package frozen peas, rinsed to separate

1 cup fat-free mayonnaise or salad dressing

1/4 cup fat-free sour cream

1/4 cup shredded low-fat cheddar cheese

Layer spinach, garbanzo beans, water chestnuts, olives, 1 cup cheese, purple onion, and peas in a 5-quart salad bowl. Mix mayonnaise and sour cream; spread over peas, spreading to edge of bowl. Sprinkle with 1/4 cup cheese. Cover and refrigerate at least 8 hours, but no longer than 24 hours. Toss just before serving.

Magic BEANS

Best-of-the-West Pasta Salad

This salad is attractive and colorful, as well as very low in fat and high in fiber. Layer it on a lettuce-lined glass platter to serve.

Make-Ahead Salad Dressing:

8-ounce carton fat-free sour cream

16-ounce jar mild salsa

1/4 teaspoon ground cumin

1/8 teaspoon hot sauce

2 cloves garlic, minced

Pasta Salad:

16-ounce package corkscrew pasta, uncooked

Lettuce leaves

15-ounce can black beans, rinsed and drained

8 3/4-ounce can whole kernel corn, rinsed and drained

1 green bell pepper, chopped

1 red bell pepper, chopped

3 green onions, sliced

1/4 cup chopped fresh cilantro

Combine all dressing ingredients, and chill for 1 hour. (Yield: 2 3/4 cups.) Cook pasta according to package directions; drain. Rinse with cold water, and drain again. Combine pasta with 1 3/4-cups Make-Ahead Salad Dressing. Toss gently; chill for 1 hour. Spoon pasta mixture onto a lettuce-lined serving platter. Top with black beans and layers of corn, green pepper, red pepper, green onions, and cilantro. Serve with remaining salad dressing.

PREPARATION TIME:
20 MINUTES

COOKING TIME:
15 MINUTES

CHILLING TIME:
2 HOURS

NUTRIENT INFORMATION
(PER SERVING):

SERVINGS PER RECIPE:	6
SERVING SIZE:	1 1/2 CUPS
CALORIES	470
PROTEIN	21 G.
CARBOHYDRATE	92 G.
FAT	2 G.
SATURATED FAT	<1 G.
CHOLESTEROL	2 MG.
SODIUM	769 MG.
DIETARY FIBER	6 G.

% CALORIES FROM:

PROTEIN:	18%
CARBOHYDRATE:	78%
FAT:	4%

FOOD EXCHANGES:
6 STARCH
1 VEGETABLE

MAKES 6 SERVINGS.

Crunchy Rainbow Lentil Salad

PREPARATION TIME:
15 MINUTES

COOKING TIME:
25 MINUTES

COOLING TIME:
10 MINUTES

CHILLING TIME:
8 HOURS

NUTRIENT INFORMATION
(PER SERVING):

SERVINGS PER RECIPE: 6
SERVING SIZE: 1 CUP
CALORIES   239
PROTEIN   5 G.
CARBOHYDRATE   39 G.
FAT   7 G.
SATURATED FAT   1 G.
CHOLESTEROL   0 MG.
SODIUM   45 MG.
DIETARY FIBER   4 G.

% CALORIES FROM:
PROTEIN: 8%
CARBOHYDRATE: 65%
FAT: 27%

FOOD EXCHANGES:
2 STARCH
1 VEGETABLE
1 FAT

MAKES 6 SERVINGS.

In the Old Testament, it is said that Esau traded his birthright for a "potage of lentils"—they are among the oldest cultivated foods. This salad can be made the night before you need it to allow plenty of time for the lentils and vegetables to marinate in their dressing.

1/2 cup uncooked lentils
1 cup water
1 cup diced celery
1/2 cup diced onion
1 small head purple cabbage, finely chopped
1/2 cup diced green bell pepper
1/2 cup diced red bell pepper
2 large carrots, grated
3 tablespoons canola oil
1/2 cup white vinegar
1/2 cup sugar

Place lentils and water in a large saucepan; bring to a boil. Cover, reduce heat, and simmer 20 minutes or until tender. Drain well, and cool slightly. Combine lentils with remaining ingredients. Chill for 8 hours.

Magic BEANS

FULL OF BEANS

Main Dishes

Santa Fe Stack-Ups

This easy-to-prepare dish provides a healthy serving of fiber.

5 corn tortillas

Nonstick cooking spray

1/2 pound ground turkey

15-ounce can pinto beans, rinsed and drained

14-1/2 ounce can no-added-salt whole tomatoes, undrained and chopped

3 tablespoons no-added-salt tomato paste

1 tablespoon chili powder

3/4 teaspoon ground cumin

1/2 teaspoon oregano

1/2 teaspoon cilantro

1/4 teaspoon salt

2 cups hot cooked brown rice

1/2 cup shredded low-fat Monterey Jack cheese

1/4 cup sliced green onions

Cut each tortilla into 8 wedges; arrange in a single layer on a baking sheet. Bake at 400° for 10 minutes or until crisp; set aside. Coat a large nonstick skillet with cooking spray, then place over medium-high heat until hot. Add turkey. Cook until browned, stirring to crumble. Remove from heat; add beans, tomatoes, tomato paste, chili powder, cumin, oregano, cilantro, and salt. Bring to a boil. Reduce heat; simmer, uncovered, 10 minutes or until thickened, stirring occasionally. Spoon rice onto serving platter; top with turkey mixture, cheese, and onions. Arrange tortilla chips around outside edge of platter.

PREPARATION TIME:
10 MINUTES

COOKING TIME:
25 MINUTES

NUTRIENT INFORMATION
(PER SERVING):

SERVINGS PER RECIPE: 4
SERVING SIZE: 10 TORTILLA
         CHIPS WITH TOPPINGS

CALORIES	497
PROTEIN	30 G.
CARBOHYDRATE	74 G.
FAT	9 G.
SATURATED FAT	2 G.
CHOLESTEROL	50 MG.
SODIUM	320 MG.
DIETARY FIBER	12 G.

% CALORIES FROM:

PROTEIN:	24%
CARBOHYDRATE:	60%
FAT:	16%

FOOD EXCHANGES:

4 STARCH

2 LEAN MEAT

2 VEGETABLE

MAKES 4 SERVINGS.

Microwave Taco Casserole

PREPARATION TIME:
10 MINUTES

COOKING TIME:
12 MINUTES

NUTRIENT INFORMATION
(PER SERVING):

SERVINGS PER RECIPE: 6
SERVING SIZE: 1 1/2 CUPS
CALORIES   383
PROTEIN   36 G.
CARBOHYDRATE   35 G.
FAT   11 G.
SATURATED FAT   5 G.
CHOLESTEROL   58 MG.
SODIUM   295 MG.
DIETARY FIBER   7 G.

% CALORIES FROM:
PROTEIN: 38%
CARBOHYDRATE: 37%
FAT: 25%

FOOD EXCHANGES:
2 STARCH
4 VERY LEAN MEAT
1 VEGETABLE
1 FAT

MAKES 6 SERVINGS.

This quick one-dish meal is a family favorite. Add more zip by using hot instead of mild salsa.

1 pound ground beef

1/2 cup chopped onion

15-ounce can pinto beans, rinsed and drained

8-ounce can no-added-salt tomato sauce

1/4 cup mild salsa

1 teaspoon chili powder

1/2 teaspoon ground cumin

1 1/2 cups shredded low-fat Monterey Jack or mozzarella cheese

2 cups broken baked tortilla chips

1 cup shredded lettuce

1/4 cup sliced green onions

1/4 cup sliced ripe olives

8-ounce container fat-free sour cream

Crumble meat into a 1 1/2-quart microwave-safe casserole; stir in chopped onion. Cover; cook on high for 4 to 5 minutes or until meat is no longer pink, stirring once. Drain off fat. Add pinto beans, tomato sauce, salsa, chili powder, and cumin. Cover; cook on high about 6 minutes or until bubbly. Top with shredded cheese. Cook, uncovered, on high about 1 minute more or until cheese melts. Top with broken tortilla chips and lettuce. Garnish with green onions, olives, and sour cream.

Magic BEANS

Vegetable Bean Pie

This is a variation of shepherd's pie, an English dish made with ground beef and topped with potatoes. Kidney beans make a wonderful meat substitute in this recipe.

4 servings instant mashed potatoes

2 tablespoons diet margarine

2 cloves garlic, minced

1/2 teaspoon basil

1/2 teaspoon thyme

1/4 teaspoon salt

3 tablespoons 2% milk

2 teaspoons olive oil

1 medium onion, chopped

1 medium carrot, sliced

15-ounce can kidney beans, rinsed and drained

14-1/2 ounce can no-added-salt diced tomatoes, undrained

10-ounce package frozen whole kernel corn

8-ounce can no-added-salt tomato sauce

1 teaspoon Worcestershire sauce

1/2 teaspoon sugar

1 cup shredded low-fat cheddar cheese

Prepare instant mashed potatoes according to package directions, and set aside. Melt margarine in a small saucepan. Cook garlic, basil, and thyme in melted margarine for 15 seconds. Add to mashed potatoes along with salt. Gradually beat in milk until potatoes are light and fluffy. For filling, heat olive oil in a large skillet. Cook and stir onion and carrot in hot oil until onion is tender. Stir in kidney beans, tomatoes, frozen corn, tomato sauce, Worcestershire sauce, and sugar; bring to boiling. Transfer to 8" x 8" baking pan. Drop mashed potatoes in 4 mounds onto the vegetable mixture. Sprinkle with cheese. Bake, uncovered, at 375° for 25 minutes or until heated through and cheese begins to brown.

PREPARATION TIME:
15 MINUTES

COOKING TIME:
30 MINUTES

NUTRIENT INFORMATION
(PER SERVING):

SERVINGS PER RECIPE:	4
SERVING SIZE:	1/4 PIE
CALORIES	421
PROTEIN	21 G.
CARBOHYDRATE	55 G.
FAT	13 G.
SATURATED FAT	4 G.
CHOLESTEROL	22 MG.
SODIUM	759 MG.
DIETARY FIBER	10 G.

% CALORIES FROM:

PROTEIN:	20%
CARBOHYDRATE:	52%
FAT:	28%

FOOD EXCHANGES:

3 STARCH

1 MEDIUM-FAT MEAT

2 VEGETABLE

2 FAT

MAKES 4 SERVINGS.

Black Bean, Sweet Potato, Turkey Salad

PREPARATION TIME:
20 MINUTES

COOKING TIME:
40 MINUTES

NUTRIENT INFORMATION
(PER SERVING):

SERVINGS PER RECIPE:	4
SERVING SIZE:	1 1/2 CUPS
CALORIES	408
PROTEIN	26 G.
CARBOHYDRATE	58 G.
FAT	8 G.
SATURATED FAT	1 G.
CHOLESTEROL	47 MG.
SODIUM	222 MG.
DIETARY FIBER	9 G.

% CALORIES FROM:

PROTEIN:	25%
CARBOHYDRATE:	57%
FAT:	18%

FOOD EXCHANGES:
3 STARCH
2 VERY LEAN MEAT
2 VEGETABLE
1 FAT

MAKES 4 SERVINGS.

This salad is a great way to use Thanksgiving leftovers!

2 medium sweet potatoes (about 1 1/4 pounds), peeled and cut into 1-inch chunks

2 teaspoons olive oil

1/2 teaspoon pepper

1/2 teaspoon chili powder

8 ounces skinless white meat turkey, cut into 1-inch pieces

2 stalks celery, thinly sliced

3/4 cup canned black beans, rinsed and drained

3 cups chicory, torn into bite-sized pieces

3 cups romaine lettuce, torn into bite-sized pieces

4 green onions, thinly sliced

Vinaigrette:

2 tablespoons chopped green chiles

1/4 cup chopped cilantro

3 tablespoons orange juice

3 tablespoons red wine vinegar

1 tablespoon plus 1 teaspoon olive oil

1/8 teaspoon pepper

Preheat oven to 400°. Place sweet potatoes in a medium bowl, and toss with olive oil. Add pepper and chili powder, and toss to coat. Spread potatoes evenly on a baking sheet. Bake 40 minutes, turning once after 20 minutes.

Meanwhile, combine all vinaigrette ingredients in a small jar with a tight fitting lid, and shake well.

Place turkey, celery, and beans in a medium bowl, and add 3 tablespoons of vinaigrette. Toss to coat, and let stand while potatoes cook. When potatoes are browned and crisp, remove from oven. Place chicory and romaine in a large serving bowl, and toss with remaining vinaigrette. Top with turkey mixture and potatoes, and sprinkle with green onions.

Magic BEANS

Beefy Bean Burritos

In this tasty recipe, beef is used as a condiment instead of the main ingredient. Serve with salsa and a salad on the side.

Nonstick cooking spray
1/2 pound beef round steak, cut into 1/2-inch pieces
2 cloves garlic, minced
15-ounce can pinto beans, rinsed and drained
4-ounce can diced green chiles, drained
1/4 cup fresh cilantro
1/4 teaspoon ground cumin
1/2 teaspoon chili powder
6 flour tortillas
1/2 cup shredded low-fat cheddar cheese

Spray a nonstick skillet with cooking spray; heat over medium heat until hot. Add steak and garlic. Cook and stir 5 minutes or until steak is cooked to desired doneness. Stir beans, chiles, cilantro, cumin, and chili powder into skillet; cook and stir 5 minutes or until heated through. Spoon steak mixture evenly down the center of each tortilla; sprinkle cheese evenly over each tortilla. Roll up, and serve.

PREPARATION TIME:
10 MINUTES

COOKING TIME:
10 MINUTES

NUTRIENT INFORMATION
(PER SERVING):
SERVINGS PER RECIPE: 6
SERVING SIZE: 1 BURRITO
CALORIES   322
PROTEIN   19 G.
CARBOHYDRATE   39 G.
FAT   10 G.
SATURATED FAT   4 G.
CHOLESTEROL   30 MG.
SODIUM   401 MG.
DIETARY FIBER   6 G.

% CALORIES FROM:
PROTEIN: 24%
CARBOHYDRATE: 48%
FAT: 28%

FOOD EXCHANGES:
2 STARCH
2 MEDIUM-FAT MEAT
1 VEGETABLE

MAKES 6 SERVINGS.

Black-Eyed Chicken Salad

PREPARATION TIME:
10 MINUTES

CHILLING TIME:
4 HOURS

NUTRIENT INFORMATION
(PER SERVING):

SERVINGS PER RECIPE:	6
SERVING SIZE:	1 CUP
CALORIES	284
PROTEIN	31 G.
CARBOHYDRATE	31 G.
FAT	4 G.
SATURATED FAT	1 G.
CHOLESTEROL	48 MG.
SODIUM	288 MG.
DIETARY FIBER	16 G.

% CALORIES FROM:

PROTEIN:	44%
CARBOHYDRATE:	44%
FAT:	13%

FOOD EXCHANGES:
2 STARCH
4 VERY LEAN MEAT

MAKES 6 SERVINGS.

Chicken breasts and black-eyed peas give this very low-fat chilled salad a double dose of protein.

16-ounce cans black-eyed peas, rinsed and drained
2 cups chopped cooked chicken breast
3/4 cup diced celery
1/2 cup chopped red bell pepper
1/2 cup chopped green bell pepper
1/2 cup sliced green onions
1/2 cup cilantro
3 tablespoons fat-free Italian salad dressing
2 tablespoons Dijon mustard
3 cups lettuce leaves

Combine all ingredients except lettuce in a bowl. Stir well. Cover and chill at least 4 hours. Serve on lettuce leaves.

Magic BEANS

Favorite Chili Macaroni

This is a classic, family-pleasing recipe that uses kidney beans to extend the ground beef and lower the fat content

1 pound ground beef

1/2 cup chopped onion

1/2 cup chopped green bell pepper

1/2 cup chopped red bell pepper

2 cloves garlic, minced

2 cups cooked elbow macaroni

1/2 cup water

1 tablespoon chili powder

1 teaspoon ground cumin

1 teaspoon fresh cilantro

1/2 teaspoon salt

1/4 teaspoon pepper

14 1/2-ounce can no-added-salt whole tomatoes, undrained and chopped

15-ounce can kidney beans, rinsed and drained

8 3/4-ounce can no-added-salt whole kernel corn, drained

8-ounce can no-added-salt tomato sauce

6-ounce can no-added-salt tomato paste

1 cup shredded low-fat cheddar cheese

Cook ground beef, onion, bell peppers, and garlic in a large Dutch oven over medium-high heat until browned, stirring to crumble beef. Drain well; wipe drippings from pan with paper towels. Return beef mixture to pan. Add all remaining ingredients except cheese, and stir well. Bring to a boil. Cover, reduce heat, and simmer 20 minutes, stirring occasionally. Spoon onto individual serving plates; top with cheese.

PREPARATION TIME:
15 MINUTES

COOKING TIME:
35 MINUTES

NUTRIENT INFORMATION
(PER SERVING):

SERVINGS PER RECIPE:	8
SERVING SIZE:	1 1/2 CUPS
CALORIES	326
PROTEIN	23 G.
CARBOHYDRATE	36 G.
FAT	10 G.
SATURATED FAT	4 G.
CHOLESTEROL	46 MG.
SODIUM	386 MG.
DIETARY FIBER	6 G.

% CALORIES FROM:

PROTEIN:	28%
CARBOHYDRATE:	44%
FAT:	28%

FOOD EXCHANGES:
2 STARCH
2 MEDIUM-FAT MEAT
1 VEGETABLE

MAKES 8 SERVINGS.

Turkey Bean Bake

PREPARATION TIME:
15 MINUTES

COOKING TIME:
75 MINUTES

STANDING TIME:
5 MINUTES

NUTRIENT INFORMATION
(PER SERVING):

SERVINGS PER RECIPE: 6
SERVING SIZE: 1 3 1/2 INCH
                        SQUARE
CALORIES   250
PROTEIN   23 G.
CARBOHYDRATE   26 G.
FAT   6 G.
SATURATED FAT   1 G.
CHOLESTEROL   37 MG.
SODIUM   897 MG.
DIETARY FIBER   4 G.

% CALORIES FROM:
PROTEIN: 37%
CARBOHYDRATE: 42%
FAT: 21%

FOOD EXCHANGES:
2 STARCH
2 LEAN MEAT

MAKES 6 SERVINGS.

After you put this dish together, let your oven do the work while you relax until supper.

1/2 pound ground turkey

1 cup chopped onion

1 3/4 teaspoons ground cumin

1 1/2 teaspoons oregano

1/2 teaspoon garlic powder

1/2 teaspoon cilantro

1/4 teaspoon pepper

16-ounce can fat-free refried beans

2 4-ounce cans diced green chiles, drained

1 cup shredded low-fat Monterey Jack cheese

1 cup frozen whole kernel corn, thawed and drained

1/3 cup flour

1 1/3 cups skim milk

1/8 teaspoon hot sauce

1/2 cup egg substitute, slightly beaten

2 egg whites

Salsa

Cook turkey and onion in a nonstick skillet over medium-high heat until browned, stirring to crumble. Combine turkey mixture, cumin, oregano, garlic powder, cilantro, pepper, and refried beans in a bowl. Stir well, and set aside. Spread half of the diced green chiles in an 11" x 7" baking dish; top with half the cheese. Spoon mounds of turkey and bean mixture onto cheese and spread gently, leaving a 1/4 inch border around edge of dish; top with corn. Spread remaining chiles over corn; top with remaining cheese. Set aside. Put flour in a bowl; gradually add milk and hot sauce, stirring until blended. Stir in egg substitute and egg whites; pour over casserole. Bake at 350° for 65 minutes or until set. Let stand 5 minutes. Garnish with salsa.

Confetti Paella

Fresh asparagus means spring is here! This colorful dish is delicious and cholesterol-free, thanks to nature's bounty.

1 pound asparagus, cut into 2-inch pieces

3 cups broccoli florets

2 teaspoons olive oil

1/2 cup chopped red bell pepper

1/2 cup chopped green bell pepper

2 small zucchini, chopped

1 medium onion, chopped

4 cups cooked brown rice

1/2 teaspoon salt

1/4 teaspoon thyme

2 large tomatoes, seeded and chopped

16-ounce cans garbanzo beans, rinsed and drained

2 10-ounce package frozen green peas, thawed

Cook asparagus and broccoli in boiling water about 4 minutes or until crisp-tender; drain. Heat oil in a large skillet over medium-high heat. Cook asparagus, broccoli, peppers, zucchini, and onion in oil about 5 minutes, stirring occasionally, until onion is crisp-tender. Stir in rice, salt, thyme, tomatoes, garbanzo beans, and peas. Cook about 5 minutes, stirring frequently, until hot.

PREPARATION TIME:
10 MINUTES

COOKING TIME:
15 MINUTES

NUTRIENT INFORMATION
(PER SERVING):

SERVINGS PER RECIPE:	6
SERVING SIZE:	1 1/2 CUPS
CALORIES	454
PROTEIN	20 G.
CARBOHYDRATE	80 G.
FAT	6 G.
SATURATED FAT	1 G.
CHOLESTEROL	0 MG.
SODIUM	622 MG.
DIETARY FIBER	17 G.

% CALORIES FROM:

PROTEIN:	18%
CARBOHYDRATE:	70%
FAT:	12%

FOOD EXCHANGES:
4 STARCH
4 VEGETABLE
1 FAT

MAKES 6 SERVINGS.

Popeye's Bean Lasagna

PREPARATION TIME:
15 MINUTES

COOKING TIME:
85 MINUTES

NUTRIENT INFORMATION
(PER SERVING):

SERVINGS PER RECIPE:	8
SERVING SIZE:	1 1/2 CUPS
CALORIES	407
PROTEIN	21 G.
CARBOHYDRATE	56 G.
FAT	11 G.
SATURATED FAT	4 G.
CHOLESTEROL	22 MG.
SODIUM	183 MG.
DIETARY FIBER	13 G.

% CALORIES FROM:

PROTEIN:	21%
CARBOHYDRATE:	55%
FAT:	24%

FOOD EXCHANGES:
3 STARCH
1 MEDIUM-FAT MEAT
2 VEGETABLE
1 FAT

MAKES 8 SERVINGS.

This variation of the usual meat-based lasagna is scrumptious. Serve with a crisp salad and Italian rolls.

2 15-ounce cans kidney beans, rinsed and drained
1 3/4 cups water
27 1/2-ounce jar no-added-salt spaghetti sauce
1 teaspoon oregano
1 teaspoon basil
10-ounce package frozen chopped spinach, thawed
    and drained
15-ounce container part-skim ricotta cheese
1/4 cup egg substitute
Nonstick cooking spray
10 uncooked lasagna noodles
1 cup shredded low-fat mozzarella cheese
1/4 cup grated Parmesan cheese

Put kidney beans in a food processor. Blend, adding water gradually, until beans are coarsely chopped. Combine bean mixture, spaghetti sauce, oregano, and basil in a saucepan; bring to a boil. Reduce heat and simmer, stirring occasionally, 10 minutes; set aside. Combine spinach, ricotta cheese, and egg substitute; set aside. Coat a 13" x 9" baking dish with cooking spray. Spread a thin layer of sauce on bottom of the dish. Arrange 5 noodles over sauce. Spread half of spinach-cheese mixture over noodles; top with mozzarella cheese. Spoon half of sauce over cheese. Repeat noodle, spinach, and sauce layers. Cover and bake at 350° for 1 hour. Uncover, sprinkle with Parmesan cheese, and bake an additional 15 minutes.

 BEANS

Tropical Black Beans and Rice

Tracking down fresh papaya is worth the effort. It will impart a special touch to everyday black beans and rice.

2 teaspoons olive oil

1/2 cup finely chopped red onion

1/2 cup orange juice

1/4 cup lemon juice

2 tablespoons chopped fresh cilantro

1/2 teaspoon cayenne pepper

1/2 cup finely chopped red bell pepper

1/2 cup finely chopped green bell pepper

1 medium papaya, peeled, seeded, and diced

2 cloves garlic, minced

2 15-ounce cans black beans, rinsed and drained

5 cups hot cooked rice

Heat oil in a large skillet over medium heat. Add all ingredients except beans and rice. Cook for 5 minutes, stirring occasionally until bell peppers are crisp-tender. Stir in beans. Cook about 5 minutes or until heated through. Serve over rice.

PREPARATION TIME:
15 MINUTES

COOKING TIME:
10 MINUTES

NUTRIENT INFORMATION
(PER SERVING):

SERVINGS PER RECIPE:	6
SERVING SIZE:	1 1/2 CUPS
CALORIES	436
PROTEIN	18 G.
CARBOHYDRATE	82 G.
FAT	4 G.
SATURATED FAT	1 G.
CHOLESTEROL	0 MG.
SODIUM	12 MG.
DIETARY FIBER	10 G.

% CALORIES FROM:

PROTEIN:	17%
CARBOHYDRATE:	75%
FAT:	8%

FOOD EXCHANGES:
4 STARCH
2 VEGETABLE
1 FRUIT

MAKES 6 SERVINGS.

Pinto-Packed Stuffed Peppers

PREPARATION TIME:
15 MINUTES

COOKING TIME:
30 MINUTES

NUTRIENT INFORMATION
(PER SERVING):

SERVINGS PER RECIPE: 6
SERVING SIZE: 1 STUFFED
                        PEPPER
CALORIES   261
PROTEIN   13 G.
CARBOHYDRATE   41 G.
FAT   5 G.
SATURATED FAT   2 G.
CHOLESTEROL   10 MG.
SODIUM   345 MG.
DIETARY FIBER   8 G.

% CALORIES FROM:
PROTEIN: 20%
CARBOHYDRATE: 63%
FAT: 17%

FOOD EXCHANGES:
2 STARCH
2 VEGETABLE
1 FAT

MAKES 6 SERVINGS.

Pinto beans provide the texture and heartiness traditionally associated with ground beef in this favorite dish.

6 medium green bell peppers
15-ounce can pinto beans, rinsed and drained
3 cups frozen whole kernel corn
3/4 cup shredded low-fat cheddar cheese
2 teaspoons olive oil
1/2 cup chopped onion
1 clove garlic, minced
1/4 cup chopped fresh parsley
1/8 teaspoon cayenne pepper
1/2 teaspoon chili powder
1/2 teaspoon ground cumin
1/4 teaspoon black pepper
Nonstick cooking spray
1/4 cup water

Cut tops off green peppers, leaving a hole about 2 inches in diameter; remove seeds and inner ribs. In a medium bowl, combine pinto beans, corn, cheese, olive oil, onion, garlic, parsley, cayenne pepper, chili powder, cumin, and black pepper. Mix thoroughly. Spoon filling into peppers. Place filled peppers in a 13" x 9" baking dish sprayed with cooking spray. Add 1/4 cup water to the baking dish, cover with foil, and bake at 375° for 20 minutes. Remove foil, and continue baking 10 minutes or until peppers are tender.

Magic BEANS

Lentil Pita Treat

Lentils are the "fast food" of the legume family. They need no soaking and require only a short cooking time.

1/2 cup lentils, uncooked

1/4 cup brown rice, uncooked

1 1/2 cups water

1/2 cup chopped green onions

1 medium peeled and shredded carrot

1/2 cup seeded and chopped cucumber

1/2 cup seeded and chopped tomato

1/2 cup fat-free ranch salad dressing

1 teaspoon basil

1 teaspoon parsley

1 clove garlic, minced

2 cups salad greens, chopped or torn

2 large whole wheat pita breads, halved and opened
   into pockets

Rinse lentils to remove dust. In a small saucepan, combine lentils, rice, and water. Cook over high heat until boiling, then reduce heat, cover, and simmer 20 minutes. Drain, and cool slightly. Stir in green onions, carrot, cucumber, tomato, dressing, basil, parsley, and garlic. Chill several hours or overnight. Add to salad greens. Spoon mixture into pita pockets to serve.

PREPARATION TIME:
10 MINUTES

COOKING TIME:
25 MINUTES

CHILLING TIME:
8 HOURS

NUTRIENT INFORMATION
(PER SERVING):

SERVINGS PER RECIPE:	4
SERVING SIZE:	1/2 FILLED PITA POCKET
CALORIES	273
PROTEIN	11 G.
CARBOHYDRATE	55 G.
FAT	1 G.
SATURATED FAT	<1 G.
CHOLESTEROL	0 MG.
SODIUM	498 MG.
DIETARY FIBER	3 G.

% CALORIES FROM:

PROTEIN:	16%
CARBOHYDRATE:	80%
FAT:	4%

FOOD EXCHANGES:
3 STARCH
1 VEGETABLE

MAKES 4 SERVINGS.

Coronado Casserole

PREPARATION TIME:
10 MINUTES

COOKING TIME:
40 MINUTES

NUTRIENT INFORMATION
(PER SERVING):

SERVINGS PER RECIPE: 4
SERVING SIZE: 1 1/2 CUPS
CALORIES   580
PROTEIN   36 G.
CARBOHYDRATE   82 G.
FAT   12 G.
SATURATED FAT   4 G.
CHOLESTEROL   54 MG.
SODIUM   980 MG.
DIETARY FIBER   14 G.

% CALORIES FROM:

PROTEIN: 25%
CARBOHYDRATE: 57%
FAT: 18%

FOOD EXCHANGES:

5 STARCH
2 MEDIUM-FAT MEAT
2 VEGETABLE

MAKES 4 SERVINGS.

If you want to assemble this casserole ahead of time, prepare everything except the cornmeal topping. Cover and chill in the refrigerator. When you're ready to cook, let the casserole stand at room temperature for 30 minutes. Add the cornmeal topping, and bake as directed.

3/4 pound ground beef

1 cup chopped onion

1 clove garlic, minced

Nonstick cooking spray

1 tablespoon chili powder

1 1/2 teaspoons ground cumin

1/2 teaspoon cilantro

1 teaspoon sugar

1/2 teaspoon oregano

2 8-ounce cans no-added-salt tomato sauce

16-ounce can pinto beans, rinsed and drained

4-ounce can diced green chiles, drained

Cornmeal Topping:

3/4 cup skim milk

1/4 cup egg substitute, slightly beaten

1 1/3 cups self-rising yellow cornmeal mix

Coat a large skillet with cooking spray. Add ground beef, onion, and garlic, and cook over medium-high heat until browned, stirring frequently to crumble the meat. Drain the fat. Add chili powder, cumin, cilantro, sugar, oregano, tomato sauce, beans, and chiles. Cover and cook over medium-low heat for 10 minutes. Pour mixture into a 2-quart casserole coated with cooking spray. Combine the milk and egg substitute in a bowl, and stir well. Add the cornmeal mix, and stir well. Pour the cornmeal mixture over the beef mixture. Bake at 400° for 20 minutes or until the cornmeal topping is lightly browned.

Magic BEANS

Hearty Mexican Potatoes

Ground beef and tasty toppings make these potatoes the main part of a meal.

4 medium baking potatoes

1/4 cup water

1/2 pound ground beef

1 small onion, chopped

15-ounce can chunky chili

1 cup canned kidney beans, rinsed and drained

4-ounce can diced green chiles, drained

1 teaspoon chili powder

1/2 teaspoon ground cumin

1 clove garlic, minced

4 cups shredded lettuce

1 tomato, chopped

1/4 cup sliced green onions

1/2 cup shredded low-fat cheddar cheese

Wash potatoes. Cut into 1/2-inch slices. Place slices in a 2-quart microwave casserole dish. Add water. Cover, and microwavable on high for 14 to 16 minutes or until potatoes are tender, stirring once. Drain. Remove potatoes from casserole dish; keep warm. Crumble meat into same casserole; stir in onion. Cover, and cook on high for 3 to 4 minutes or until meat is no longer pink and onion is tender, stirring once. Drain off fat. Stir in chili, beans, green chiles, chili powder, cumin, and garlic. Cover, and cook on high for 6 to 8 minutes or until heated through, stirring twice. Arrange 1 cup of shredded lettuce on each of 4 plates. Place potato slices over lettuce; spoon meat and bean mixture on top. Sprinkle with chopped tomato, green onions, and shredded cheese.

PREPARATION TIME:
10 MINUTES

COOKING TIME:
25 MINUTES

NUTRIENT INFORMATION
(PER SERVING):
SERVINGS PER RECIPE: 4
SERVING SIZE: 1 POTATO WITH
                            TOPPING

CALORIES	588
PROTEIN	31 G.
CARBOHYDRATE	80 G.
FAT	16 G.
SATURATED FAT	7 G.
CHOLESTEROL	64 MG.
SODIUM	907 MG.
DIETARY FIBER	13 G.

% CALORIES FROM:
PROTEIN:	21%
CARBOHYDRATE:	55%
FAT:	24%

FOOD EXCHANGES:
5 STARCH
2 MEDIUM-FAT MEAT
1 VEGETABLE
1 FAT

MAKES 4 SERVINGS.

Vegetable Stew

PREPARATION TIME:
5 MINUTES

COOKING TIME:
30 MINUTES

NUTRIENT INFORMATION
(PER SERVING):
SERVINGS PER RECIPE: 6
SERVING SIZE: 1 1/2 CUPS
CALORIES   316
PROTEIN   9 G.
CARBOHYDRATE   61 G.
FAT   4 G.
SATURATED FAT   <1 G.
CHOLESTEROL   0 MG.
SODIUM   63 MG.
DIETARY FIBER   7 G.

% CALORIES FROM:
PROTEIN: 11%
CARBOHYDRATE: 77%
FAT: 11%

FOOD EXCHANGES:
4 STARCH
1 FAT

MAKES 6 SERVINGS.

This colorful vegetable creole is served over rice.

1/2 cup diced celery

1/3 cup sliced onions

1 tablespoon olive oil

16-ounce can no-added-salt tomatoes

1 teaspoon basil

1/2 teaspoon rosemary

1 teaspoon sesame seeds

1/2 teaspoon cayenne pepper

1/4 teaspoon cilantro

10-ounce package frozen peas

1/2 cup canned dark red kidney beans, rinsed and drained

6 cups cooked brown rice

Sauté celery and onions in oil until tender. Add tomatoes, basil, rosemary, sesame seeds, pepper, and cilantro. Cook 20 minutes, stirring occasionally. Add peas and beans. Cover and cook 5 minutes longer until thoroughly heated. Serve over hot brown rice.

Magic BEANS

Micro-Rave Red Beans and Rice

For variety, any type of bean may be substituted for red beans.

2 cups chopped onions

2 cloves garlic, minced

1 bay leaf

1/4 teaspoon cayenne pepper

8-ounce can no-added-salt tomato sauce

1 teaspoon Worcestershire sauce

1/4 teaspoon hot pepper sauce

3/4 pound turkey kielbasa, cut in 1/4-inch slices

2 15-ounce cans red beans, rinsed and drained

3 cups hot cooked brown rice

Prepare rice according to package directions. Combine onions, garlic, bay leaf, cayenne pepper, tomato sauce, Worcestershire sauce, and hot pepper sauce in a 3-quart microwavable baking dish. Cover and cook on high for 6 minutes. Stir in kielbasa and beans. Cover and cook on medium for 10 minutes, stirring after 5 minutes. Remove bay leaf. Serve over hot rice.

PREPARATION TIME:
5 MINUTES

COOKING TIME:
16 MINUTES

NUTRIENT INFORMATION
(PER SERVING):

SERVINGS PER RECIPE:	6
SERVING SIZE:	1 CUP
CALORIES	418
PROTEIN	26 G.
CARBOHYDRATE	65 G.
FAT	6 G.
SATURATED FAT	1 G.
CHOLESTEROL	38 MG.
SODIUM	681 MG.
DIETARY FIBER	10 G.

% CALORIES FROM:

PROTEIN:	25%
CARBOHYDRATE:	62%
FAT:	13%

FOOD EXCHANGES:

4 STARCH

2 LEAN MEAT

1 VEGETABLE

MAKES 6 SERVINGS.

Shortcut Cassoulet

PREPARATION TIME:
15 MINUTES

COOKING TIME:
1 HOUR

NUTRIENT INFORMATION
(PER SERVING):

SERVINGS PER RECIPE:	8
SERVING SIZE:	1 1/2 CUPS
CALORIES	397
PROTEIN	24 G.
CARBOHYDRATE	54 G.
FAT	8 G.
SATURATED FAT	<1 G.
CHOLESTEROL	30 MG.
SODIUM	562 MG.
DIETARY FIBER	10 G.

% CALORIES FROM:

PROTEIN:	24%
CARBOHYDRATE:	54%
FAT:	18%
ALCOHOL:	4%

FOOD EXCHANGES:
3 STARCH
1 VERY LEAN MEAT
2 VEGETABLE
1 FAT

MAKES 8 SERVINGS.

This recipe is based on the classic French stew, which traditionally takes three days to make!

16-ounce can black beans, rinsed and drained
16-ounce can navy beans, rinsed and drained
16-ounce can dark red kidney beans, rinsed and drained
1 pound turkey kielbasa, sliced into 1-inch pieces
15-ounce can no-added-salt tomato sauce
1 1/2 cups thinly sliced carrots
2 small onions, thinly sliced, and separated into rings
1/2 cup dry red wine
2 tablespoons firmly packed brown sugar
1 1/2 teaspoons thyme
2 cloves garlic, finely chopped
1 bay leaf
1/2 teaspoon black pepper
1 tablespoon minced fresh parsley

Preheat oven to 375°. Mix all ingredients in an ungreased 3-quart casserole dish. Cover, and bake about 1 hour or until hot and bubbly and carrots are tender. Remove bay leaf before serving.

Magic BEANS

Best Black Bean and Rice Burritos

These low-fat burritos have an excellent flavor. You can substitute kidney or pinto beans for black beans for a variation.

1 bag boil-in-bag brown rice

1 tablespoon Mrs. Dash garlic and herb spice blend

1/4 teaspoon ground cumin

1 teaspoon cilantro

15-ounce can black beans, undrained

6 flour tortillas

3/4 cup shredded low-fat sharp cheddar cheese

1/4 cup plus 2 tablespoons sliced green onions

1/4 cup plus 2 tablespoons mild salsa

1/4 cup plus 2 tablespoons plain low-fat yogurt

Cook rice according to package directions, omitting salt and fat. Combine Mrs. Dash, cumin, cilantro, and black beans in a medium saucepan; bring to a boil. Reduce heat and simmer, uncovered, 5 minutes, stirring occasionally. Remove from heat, and stir in rice. Spoon about 1/3 cup bean mixture down the center of each tortilla. Top each with 2 tablespoons cheese, 1 tablespoon green onions, 1 tablespoon salsa, and 1 tablespoon yogurt. Roll up, and serve.

PREPARATION TIME:
5 MINUTES

COOKING TIME:
10 MINUTES

NUTRIENT INFORMATION
(PER SERVING):

SERVINGS PER RECIPE:	6
SERVING SIZE:	1 BURRITO
CALORIES	313
PROTEIN	16 G.
CARBOHYDRATE	51 G.
FAT	5 G.
SATURATED FAT	2 G.
CHOLESTEROL	11 MG.
SODIUM	362 MG.
DIETARY FIBER	4 G.

% CALORIES FROM:

PROTEIN:	20%
CARBOHYDRATE:	65%
FAT:	15%

FOOD EXCHANGES:
3 STARCH
1 MEDIUM-FAT MEAT
1 VEGETABLE

MAKES 6 SERVINGS.

Turkey-Pinto-Orzo Skillet

PREPARATION TIME:
5 MINUTES

COOKING TIME:
25 MINUTES

NUTRIENT INFORMATION
(PER SERVING):

SERVINGS PER RECIPE: 4
SERVING SIZE: 1 1/2 CUPS
CALORIES   426
PROTEIN   33 G.
CARBOHYDRATE   51 G.
FAT   10 G.
SATURATED FAT   3 G.
CHOLESTEROL   91 MG.
SODIUM   562 MG.
DIETARY FIBER   10 G.

% CALORIES FROM:
PROTEIN: 31%
CARBOHYDRATE: 48%
FAT: 21%

FOOD EXCHANGES:
3 STARCH
3 LEAN MEAT
1 VEGETABLE

MAKES 4 SERVINGS.

Orzo, also known as rosamarina, is a tiny, rice-shaped pasta. Keep it handy on the pantry shelf to use in quick, one-dish meals such as this. Garnish with fat-free sour cream, if desired.

1 pound ground turkey
1 1/2 cups medium salsa
1/2 cup uncooked orzo pasta
1 cup water
1/2 cup chopped green bell pepper
1 tablespoon chopped fresh cilantro
1/2 teaspoon chili powder
1/8 teaspoon hot sauce
16-ounce can pinto beans, rinsed and drained

Cook ground turkey in a large skillet over medium heat, stirring occasionally, until browned. Drain. Stir in remaining ingredients. Heat to boiling; reduce heat. Cover and simmer about 15 minutes, stirring frequently, until pasta is tender.

Magic BEANS

Lamb and Lentil Casserole

This hearty casserole includes quick-cooking lentils. Serve with crusty French bread and garden salad.

2 slices bacon, cut into 1-inch pieces

1 tablespoon olive oil

1 pound lamb, cut into 3/4-inch pieces

1 cup uncooked lentils, rinsed

1 cup water

1 tablespoon firmly packed brown sugar

1 tablespoon chopped fresh thyme

1 tablespoon chopped fresh savory

1/4 teaspoon salt

1/4 teaspoon pepper

3 medium carrots, thinly sliced

1 large onion, sliced

14 1/2-ounce can no-added-salt stewed tomatoes, undrained

8-ounce can no-added-salt tomato sauce

Heat oven to 350°. Cook bacon in a skillet over medium heat, stirring occasionally, until crisp. Drain and pat dry. Heat olive oil in a Dutch oven over medium heat. Cook lamb in oil, stirring frequently, until brown; drain. Stir in bacon and remaining ingredients. Heat to boiling, then remove from heat. Spoon into an ungreased 2-quart casserole. Cover and bake 55 minutes, stirring occasionally, until lamb and lentils are tender.

PREPARATION TIME:
15 MINUTES

COOKING TIME:
80 MINUTES

NUTRIENT INFORMATION
(PER SERVING):

SERVINGS PER RECIPE:	4
SERVING SIZE:	1 1/2 CUPS
CALORIES	464
PROTEIN	36 G.
CARBOHYDRATE	53 G.
FAT	12 G.
SATURATED FAT	4 G.
CHOLESTEROL	83 MG.
SODIUM	445 MG.
DIETARY FIBER	7 G.

% CALORIES FROM:

PROTEIN:	31%
CARBOHYDRATE:	46%
FAT:	23%

FOOD EXCHANGES:
3 STARCH
3 LEAN MEAT
2 VEGETABLE
1 FAT

MAKES 4 SERVINGS.

Fettuccine With Hot Mexican Bean Sauce

PREPARATION TIME:
10 MINUTES

COOKING TIME:
25 MINUTES

NUTRIENT INFORMATION
(PER SERVING):
SERVINGS PER RECIPE: 4
SERVING SIZE: 1 1/2 CUPS
CALORIES   366
PROTEIN   16 G.
CARBOHYDRATE   71 G.
FAT   2 G.
SATURATED FAT   <1 G.
CHOLESTEROL   0 MG.
SODIUM   97 MG.
DIETARY FIBER   10 G.

% CALORIES FROM:
PROTEIN: 17%
CARBOHYDRATE: 78%
FAT: 5%

FOOD EXCHANGES:
4 STARCH
3 VEGETABLE

MAKES 4 SERVINGS.

This popular recipe comes from the American Dry Bean Board.

Nonstick cooking spray

1 medium onion, chopped

1 clove garlic, minced

14 1/2-ounce can no-added-salt stewed tomatoes, undrained

10-ounce can no-added-salt tomatoes, undrained

2 tablespoons chopped green chiles

1 tablespoon chopped fresh cilantro

1 teaspoon chili powder

1/2 teaspoon sugar

1/4 teaspoon oregano

16-ounce can kidney beans, rinsed and drained

4 cups hot cooked fettuccine, cooked without salt

Coat a large skillet with cooking spray. Place over medium heat until hot. Add onion and garlic; sauté until tender. Stir in tomatoes, green chiles, cilantro, chili powder, sugar, and oregano. Cover and bring to a boil. Reduce heat, and simmer 15 minutes, stirring occasionally. Mash beans slightly, and stir into tomato mixture. Serve over hot cooked fettuccine.

Magic BEANS

Fiesta Chicken

A healthy and tasty answer to the eternal question, "What's for supper?"

- 1/2 cup flour
- 1/2 teaspoon garlic powder
- 1/4 teaspoon chili powder
- 2 1/2 pounds skinless, boneless chicken breasts
- 1 tablespoon olive oil
- 15-ounce can black beans, rinsed and drained
- 14 1/2-ounce can diced tomatoes, undrained
- 4-ounce can diced green chiles, drained
- 1/2 cup chopped green pepper
- 1/2 cup chopped onion
- 1/2 cup sliced olives
- 1/8 teaspoon garlic powder
- 2 cups hot cooked rice

Combine flour, 1/2 teaspoon garlic powder, and chili powder in a paper or plastic bag. Shake chicken breasts, a few pieces at a time, in flour mixture until well coated. Heat olive oil in a large skillet over medium heat. Cook chicken in hot oil about 10 minutes or until chicken is lightly browned, turning to brown evenly. Drain off fat.

Combine black beans, undrained tomatoes, chiles, green pepper, onion, olives, and garlic powder in a mixing bowl; mix well. Pour bean mixture over chicken in skillet. Bring to boiling, then reduce heat. Simmer, covered, about 40 minutes or until chicken is tender and no longer pink. Serve over hot cooked rice.

PREPARATION TIME:
10 MINUTES

COOKING TIME:
50 MINUTES

NUTRIENT INFORMATION
(PER SERVING):

SERVINGS PER RECIPE:	8
SERVING SIZE:	1 1/2 CUPS
CALORIES	384
PROTEIN	43 G.
CARBOHYDRATE	35 G.
FAT	8 G.
SATURATED FAT	2 G.
CHOLESTEROL	96 MG.
SODIUM	324 MG.
DIETARY FIBER	5 G.

% CALORIES FROM:

PROTEIN:	45%
CARBOHYDRATE:	36%
FAT:	19%

FOOD EXCHANGES:
- 2 STARCH
- 5 VERY LEAN MEAT
- 1 VEGETABLE
- 1 FAT

MAKES 8 SERVINGS.

Mexican Microwave Manicotti

PREPARATION TIME:
15 MINUTES

COOKING TIME:
30 MINUTES

STANDING TIME:
5 MINUTES

NUTRIENT INFORMATION
(PER SERVING):

SERVINGS PER RECIPE: 4
SERVING SIZE: 2 STUFFED
               MANICOTTI SHELLS
CALORIES   468
PROTEIN   30 G.
CARBOHYDRATE   60 G.
FAT   12 G.
SATURATED FAT   4 G.
CHOLESTEROL   42 MG.
SODIUM   620 MG.
DIETARY FIBER   6 G.

% CALORIES FROM:
PROTEIN: 26%
CARBOHYDRATE: 51%
FAT: 23%

FOOD EXCHANGES:
4 STARCH
3 VERY LEAN MEAT
2 FAT

MAKES 4 SERVINGS.

Use the microwave to cook ground beef and beans in this one-dish meal. Serve with Spanish rice and picante sauce for added zip.

1 cup canned pinto beans, rinsed and drained

1/2 pound lean ground beef

1 teaspoon oregano

1/2 teaspoon ground cumin

8 uncooked manicotti shells

1 cup picante sauce

1 cup water

1/2 cup shredded low-fat Monterey Jack cheese

1/2 cup fat-free sour cream

1/4 cup sliced olives

2 tablespoons chopped green onion

Mash pinto beans, and combine with ground beef, oregano, and cumin; mix well. Fill uncooked manicotti shells with meat and bean mixture. Place in a 10" x 6" inch glass baking dish. Combine picante sauce and water; pour over shells. Cover with vented plastic wrap. Cook in microwave on high for 10 minutes. Using tongs, rearrange and turn shells over. Cover with vented plastic wrap. Cook on medium 18 to 20 minutes, rotating dish after 10 minutes of cooking. Sprinkle with cheese. Let stand uncovered 5 minutes. Top with sour cream, olives, and green onion.

Time-Saver Tostadas

When minutes matter, this quick dish gets to the table in less than a half hour.

4 corn tortillas
1/2 pound lean ground beef
1 cup canned kidney beans, rinsed and drained
2/3 cup frozen whole kernel corn
1/2 cup chopped red bell pepper
1/2 cup chopped green bell pepper
1/4 cup mild taco sauce
2 tablespoons sliced ripe olives
2 cups shredded lettuce
1/2 cup shredded low-fat sharp cheddar cheese
1/2 cup plain nonfat yogurt
1 chopped tomato

Arrange tortillas in a single layer on a baking sheet. Bake at 350° for 6 minutes. Turn tortillas over, and bake an additional 6 minutes or until crisp. Cool on a wire rack. Cook ground beef in a medium nonstick skillet over medium heat until browned, stirring to crumble. Drain well, and wipe drippings from skillet with a paper towel. Return meat to skillet, and add kidney beans, corn, peppers, taco sauce, and olives. Cook over medium heat 2 minutes or until thoroughly heated. To serve, top each tortilla with 1/2 cup shredded lettuce, 1/2 cup meat mixture, 2 tablespoons shredded cheese, and 2 tablespoons yogurt. Garnish with chopped tomato.

PREPARATION TIME:
5 MINUTES

COOKING TIME:
25 MINUTES

NUTRIENT INFORMATION
(PER SERVING):

SERVINGS PER RECIPE:	4
SERVING SIZE:	1 TOSTADA WITH TOPPINGS
CALORIES	339
PROTEIN	24 G.
CARBOHYDRATE	36 G.
FAT	11 G.
SATURATED FAT	4 G.
CHOLESTEROL	47 MG.
SODIUM	414 MG.
DIETARY FIBER	6 G.

% CALORIES FROM:

PROTEIN:	28%
CARBOHYDRATE:	42%
FAT:	30%

FOOD EXCHANGES:
2 STARCH
2 MEDIUM-FAT MEAT
1 VEGETABLE

MAKES 4 SERVINGS.

Chilled Tuna Bean Salad

PREPARATION TIME:
15 MINUTES

BROILING TIME:
10 MINUTES

CHILLING TIME:
4 HOURS

NUTRIENT INFORMATION
(PER SERVING):
SERVINGS PER RECIPE: 6
SERVING SIZE: 3/4 CUP TUNA
        SALAD ON LETTUCE WITH
            4 TOMATO WEDGES
CALORIES   445
PROTEIN   32 G.
CARBOHYDRATE   50 G.
FAT   13 G.
SATURATED FAT   2 G.
CHOLESTEROL   17 MG.
SODIUM   780 MG.
DIETARY FIBER   9 G.

% CALORIES FROM:
PROTEIN: 32%
CARBOHYDRATE: 38%
FAT: 29%

FOOD EXCHANGES:
2 STARCH
3 LEAN MEAT
3 VEGETABLE
1 FAT

MAKES 6 SERVINGS.

This cool salad makes a wonderful main dish on a hot summer day!

3 medium green bell peppers

2 15-ounce cans cannellini beans, rinsed and drained

2 6 1/8-ounce cans water-packed tuna, drained

1/2 cup sliced ripe olives

1 head lettuce

2 medium tomatoes, cut into wedges

Rosemary Dressing:

1/2 teaspoon grated lemon peel

1/3 cup lemon juice

1/4 cup olive oil

2 tablespoons chopped fresh parsley

1 teaspoon rosemary

1 tablespoon Dijon mustard

1/2 teaspoon salt

Mix all dressing ingredients thoroughly in a tightly covered container.

Set oven control to broil. Place bell peppers on broiler pan. Broil with tops 4 to 5 inches from heat about 5 minutes on each side or until skin blisters and browns. Remove from oven. Wrap in towel; let stand 5 minutes. Remove skin, stems, seeds, and membranes from peppers. Cut peppers into 1/4-inch slices. Toss peppers, beans, tuna, olives, and dressing in a bowl. Cover and refrigerate at least 4 hours to blend flavors, stirring occasionally. Spoon salad onto lettuce leaves. Garnish with tomato wedges.

Magic BEANS

Garden Burritos

Mushrooms and garden vegetables add texture and substance to these burritos.

Nonstick cooking spray

1 pound sliced fresh mushrooms

1 cup chopped onions

1/2 cup chopped green pepper

1/2 cup chopped red pepper

2 cloves garlic, minced

15-ounce can kidney beans, rinsed and drained

2 tablespoons finely chopped black olives

1/4 teaspoon black pepper

8 flour tortillas

1/2 cup fat-free sour cream

1 cup mild chunky salsa, divided

1/2 cup shredded low-fat cheddar cheese

Spray a large nonstick skillet with cooking spray. Cook mushrooms, onions, peppers, and garlic over medium-high heat, stirring constantly, until tender. Remove from heat; drain. Combine cooked vegetables, kidney beans, olives, and pepper. Spoon bean mixture evenly down the center of each tortilla. Top with 1 tablespoon sour cream, 1 tablespoon salsa, and 1 tablespoon cheese. Fold opposite sides over filling to seal. In a large non-stick skillet coated with cooking spray, cook tortillas over medium-high heat for 1 minute on each side, or until thoroughly heated. Top with remaining salsa.

PREPARATION TIME:
15 MINUTES

COOKING TIME:
6 MINUTES

NUTRIENT INFORMATION
(PER SERVING):

SERVINGS PER RECIPE:	8
SERVING SIZE:	1 BURRITO
CALORIES	237
PROTEIN	11 G.
CARBOHYDRATE	37 G.
FAT	5 G.
SATURATED FAT	1 G.
CHOLESTEROL	6 MG.
SODIUM	463 MG.
DIETARY FIBER	5 G.

% CALORIES FROM:

PROTEIN:	19%
CARBOHYDRATE:	62%
FAT:	19%

FOOD EXCHANGES:
1 STARCH
4 VEGETABLE
1 FAT

MAKES 8 SERVINGS.

Blue Ribbon Bean Enchiladas

PREPARATION TIME:
10 MINUTES

COOKING TIME:
25 MINUTES

NUTRIENT INFORMATION
(PER SERVING):
SERVINGS PER RECIPE: 4
SERVING SIZE: 2 ENCHILADAS
CALORIES   361
PROTEIN   22 G.
CARBOHYDRATE   48 G.
FAT   9 G.
SATURATED FAT   1 G.
CHOLESTEROL   11 MG.
SODIUM   820 MG.
DIETARY FIBER   4 G.

% CALORIES FROM:
PROTEIN: 25%
CARBOHYDRATE: 53%
FAT: 22%

FOOD EXCHANGES:
3 STARCH
2 VERY LEAN MEAT
1 FAT

MAKES 4 SERVINGS.

Enchiladas are a great alternative to high-fat mexican meals.

Quick Sauce:

1 tablespoon olive oil

1 tablespoon chili powder

1 1/2 tablespoons flour

1 1/2 cups water

1 teaspoon vinegar

1/2 teaspoon garlic powder

1/2 teaspoon onion powder

1/4 teaspoon cayenne pepper

1/4 teaspoon oregano

Enchiladas:

1/2 cup low-fat cottage cheese

3/4 cup no-added-salt refried beans

2 tablespoons chopped green chiles

1 cup shredded low-fat cheddar or Monterey Jack cheese, divided

1 medium onion, finely chopped

8 corn tortillas

1 cup fat-free sour cream

4 tablespoons chopped green onions

Sauce: Heat oil, chili powder, and flour in a small saucepan to make a paste. Add water gradually to make a smooth sauce; add vinegar, garlic powder, onion powder, pepper, and oregano. Bring to a boil. Lower heat; simmer uncovered for about 3 minutes.

Enchiladas: Preheat oven to 350°. Mix cottage cheese, beans, chiles, 2/3 cup cheese, and onion in a bowl. Warm the tortillas in the oven or microwave. Place 1/4 cup of the bean filling down the center of each tortilla. Roll up, and place seam side down in a shallow baking dish. Pour sauce over filled enchiladas, and sprinkle with remaining cheese. Bake for 20 minutes or until bubbly. Top with sour cream and green onions before serving.

 Magic BEANS

Turkey Salsa Sauté

This colorful dish takes only a few minutes to prepare.

1 teaspoon chili powder

1 teaspoon ground cumin

1/2 teaspoon salt

1/4 teaspoon cayenne pepper

1 pound turkey tenderloins

4 teaspoons olive oil

1/4 cup lime juice

1/3 cup chopped onion

4-ounce can diced green chiles, drained

15-ounce can black beans, rinsed and drained

8 3/4-ounce can corn, drained

1/3 cup chopped tomato

2 tablespoons fresh cilantro

1 lime, cut into quarters

In a small bowl, combine chili powder, cumin, salt, and cayenne pepper; sprinkle half of the mixture over turkey. In a nonstick skillet over medium-high heat, brown turkey in 2 teaspoons olive oil, 3 to 4 minutes on each side. Add lime juice, cover, and reduce heat to low. Cook 8 to 10 minutes or until meat is no longer pink in center. In a medium nonstick skillet over medium-high heat, sauté onion and green chiles in remaining oil 2 to 3 minutes or until onion softens. Add beans, corn, tomato, cilantro, and the remaining spice mixture. Cook 5 to 10 minutes or until mixture is heated throughout. To serve, squeeze lime wedge over each serving.

PREPARATION TIME:
10 MINUTES

COOKING TIME:
30 MINUTES

NUTRIENT INFORMATION
(PER SERVING):

SERVINGS PER RECIPE:	4
SERVING SIZE:	1 1/2 CUPS
CALORIES	401
PROTEIN	37 G.
CARBOHYDRATE	43 G.
FAT	9 G.
SATURATED FAT	2 G.
CHOLESTEROL	59 MG.
SODIUM	552 MG.
DIETARY FIBER	6 G.

% CALORIES FROM:

PROTEIN:	37%
CARBOHYDRATE:	43%
FAT:	20%

FOOD EXCHANGES:
3 STARCH
4 VERY LEAN MEAT
1 FAT

MAKES 4 SERVINGS.

Pronto Pita Pizzas

This fast food is good for you!

4 whole wheat pita breads
1/2 cup no-added-salt tomato sauce
1 cup canned pinto beans, rinsed, drained, and mashed
1/4 cup shredded low-fat Monterey Jack cheese
1 teaspoon oregano
1 teaspoon ground cumin

Spread tomato sauce on pita bread. Top with mashed pinto beans. Sprinkle each pita with cheese, oregano, and cumin.

Magic BEANS

Great Bean Gumbo

A hearty main dish with a southern flavor.

1 1/2 cups frozen okra

1 cup chopped onions

1 clove garlic, mashed

1 tablespoon olive oil

1/2 cup diced celery

1 medium green pepper, chopped

2 16-ounce cans no-added-salt tomatoes

1/4 teaspoon black pepper

1/4 teaspoon cayenne pepper

1 teaspoon thyme

1 cup frozen peas

16-ounce can kidney beans, rinsed and drained

3 cups cooked brown rice

Cook okra in boiling water until tender. Set aside. Sauté onions and garlic in olive oil until onion is soft and golden. Add celery and green pepper, and cook until tender. Add tomatoes, and heat to boiling. Reduce heat. Add pepper, cayenne, and thyme, and simmer for 45 minutes. Add cooked okra, peas, and beans. Cook for a few minutes longer until peas are done. Serve over hot cooked brown rice.

PREPARATION TIME:
10 MINUTES

COOKING TIME:
60 MINUTES

NUTRIENT INFORMATION
(PER SERVING):

SERVINGS PER RECIPE:	6
SERVING SIZE:	1 1/2 CUPS
CALORIES	316
PROTEIN	13 G.
CARBOHYDRATE	57 G.
FAT	4 G.
SATURATED FAT	<1 G.
CHOLESTEROL	0 MG.
SODIUM	61 MG.
DIETARY FIBER	9 G.

% CALORIES FROM:

PROTEIN:	16%
CARBOHYDRATE:	72%
FAT:	12%

FOOD EXCHANGES:
3 STARCH
3 VEGETABLE
1 FAT

MAKES 6 SERVINGS.

Mexitalian Casserole

PREPARATION TIME:
10 MINUTES

COOKING TIME:
60 MINUTES

STANDING TIME:
5 MINUTES

NUTRIENT INFORMATION
(PER SERVING):

SERVINGS PER RECIPE: 5
SERVING SIZE: 1 1/2 CUPS
CALORIES   454
PROTEIN   27 G.
CARBOHYDRATE   64 G.
FAT   10 G.
SATURATED FAT   5 G.
CHOLESTEROL   30 MG.
SODIUM   469 MG.
DIETARY FIBER   7 G.

% CALORIES FROM:
PROTEIN: 24%
CARBOHYDRATE: 56%
FAT: 20%

FOOD EXCHANGES:
3 STARCH
2 LEAN MEAT
3 VEGETABLE
1 FAT

MAKES 5 SERVINGS.

Kids love this high fiber, one-dish dinner.

4 ounces ziti pasta, uncooked
Nonstick cooking spray
2 medium onions, chopped
1 clove garlic, minced
1 medium carrot, finely chopped
16-ounce can no-added-salt tomatoes, undrained
8-ounce can no-added-salt tomato sauce
1 teaspoon oregano
16-ounce can black beans, rinsed and drained
10-ounce package frozen corn, thawed
2 tablespoons chopped green chiles
8 ounces part-skim ricotta cheese
4 ounces shredded low-fat Monterey Jack cheese

Cook ziti according to package directions without salt; drain well. Preheat oven to 375°. Coat a Dutch oven or large pot with cooking spray. Add onions, garlic, and carrot; sauté over medium heat for 10 minutes, stirring often. Stir in tomatoes, breaking them up with a spoon, then tomato sauce, and oregano. Bring to a boil. Reduce heat to low; simmer for 15 minutes or until slightly thickened. Stir in beans, corn, and chiles. Cook for 5 minutes. Remove from heat; add drained pasta and cheeses; toss gently. Spoon into a 9-inch square baking dish coated with cooking spray.

Bake for 30 minutes or until heated through. Let stand for 5 minutes before serving.

Magic BEANS

Hoppin' John

Southern folklore holds that black-eyed peas bring good luck when served on New Year's Day. Don't wait until then to enjoy this practically fat-free version of a traditional dish!

1/2 cup uncooked brown rice

1/4 cup chopped red bell pepper

1/4 cup chopped green bell pepper

1/2 cup water

1/4 teaspoon salt

1/8 teaspoon pepper

1 small zucchini, sliced

16-ounce can black-eyed peas, rinsed and drained

16-ounce can no-added-salt stewed tomatoes

2 tablespoons chopped fresh parsley

Heat all ingredients except parsley to boiling in a 2-quart saucepan; reduce heat. Cover and simmer 20 minutes. Stir in parsley just before serving.

PREPARATION TIME:
10 MINUTES

COOKING TIME:
25 MINUTES

NUTRIENT INFORMATION
(PER SERVING):

SERVINGS PER RECIPE:	4
SERVING SIZE:	1 1/2 CUPS
CALORIES	265
PROTEIN	13 G.
CARBOHYDRATE	51 G.
FAT	1 G.
SATURATED FAT	<1 G.
CHOLESTEROL	0 MG.
SODIUM	174 MG.
DIETARY FIBER	13 G.

% CALORIES FROM:

PROTEIN:	20%
CARBOHYDRATE:	77%
FAT:	3%

FOOD EXCHANGES:
3 STARCH
2 VEGETABLE

MAKES 4 SERVINGS.

Where's-the-Beef? Burgers

PREPARATION TIME:
10 MINUTES

COOKING TIME:
10 MINUTES

NUTRIENT INFORMATION
(PER SERVING):

SERVINGS PER RECIPE: 4
SERVING SIZE: 1 PATTY
CALORIES   362
PROTEIN   21 G.
CARBOHYDRATE   47 G.
FAT   10 G.
SATURATED FAT   1 G.
CHOLESTEROL   58 MG.
SODIUM   495 MG.
DIETARY FIBER   11 G.

% CALORIES FROM:
PROTEIN: 23%
CARBOHYDRATE: 52%
FAT: 25%

FOOD EXCHANGES:
3 STARCH
1 LEAN MEAT
1 FAT

MAKES 4 SERVINGS.

Serve these burgers on a toasted whole wheat hamburger bun for a tasty change from the usual cookout fare!

> 2 16-ounce cans kidney beans, rinsed and drained
> 1 large egg
> 1/4 cup seasoned bread crumbs
> 1 1/2 teaspoons Italian seasoning
> 1 1/2 tablespoons olive oil
> 1/2 cup pizza sauce
> 1/2 cup shredded low-fat mozzarella cheese

Place beans in a large bowl, and mash with a fork until chunky. Add egg, bread crumbs, and Italian seasoning. Mix well. Shape mixture into four 1/2-inch thick patties. Heat oil in a large non-stick skillet. Cook patties in skillet over medium-high heat for 3 to 4 minutes per side or until patties are heated through and slightly crusty. Reduce heat to low. Top each patty with sauce, then cheese. Cover skillet, and cook for 1 to 2 minutes or until cheese begins to melt.

Magic BEANS

Island Chicken With Black Beans

Tropical fruits and spices add a taste of the islands to this microwave chicken dish. Serve with brown rice or pasta.

- 2 pounds of chicken drumsticks or thighs
- 1 cup cubed mango or 1 8-ounce can sliced peaches, drained and diced
- 1 teaspoon ginger
- 1/4 teaspoon cloves
- 1 teaspoon finely shredded lemon peel
- 2 tablespoons lime juice
- 1/2 teaspoon salt
- 1 clove garlic, finely chopped
- 2 green onions, thinly sliced
- 2 15-ounce cans black beans, undrained

Arrange chicken pieces, skin side up and thickest parts to outside edges, in an 11" x 9" microwavable dish. Cover with plastic wrap, folding back one corner to vent. Microwave on high 9 minutes. Remove excess fat. Rotate dish a half turn. Mix remaining ingredients; spoon over and around chicken pieces. Re-cover, and microwave on high about 8 minutes longer or until juice of chicken is no longer pink when centers of thickest pieces are cut. Let stand 3 minutes before serving.

PREPARATION TIME:
10 MINUTES

COOKING TIME:
17 MINUTES

STANDING TIME:
3 MINUTES

NUTRIENT INFORMATION
(PER SERVING):

SERVINGS PER RECIPE:	6
SERVING SIZE:	2 CHICKEN PIECES
CALORIES	334
PROTEIN	30 G.
CARBOHYDRATE	40 G.
FAT	6 G.
SATURATED FAT	2 G.
CHOLESTEROL	60 MG.
SODIUM	253 MG.
DIETARY FIBER	6 G.

% CALORIES FROM:

PROTEIN:	36%
CARBOHYDRATE:	48%
FAT:	16%

FOOD EXCHANGES:
3 STARCH
3 VERY LEAN MEAT
1 FAT

MAKES 6 SERVINGS.

Rice Skillet Olé

PREPARATION TIME:
10 MINUTES

COOKING TIME:
20 MINUTES

NUTRIENT INFORMATION
PER SERVING):
SERVINGS PER RECIPE: 4
SERVING SIZE: 1 1/2 CUPS
CALORIES   455
PROTEIN   22 G.
CARBOHYDRATE   76 G.
FAT   7 G.
SATURATED FAT   1 G.
CHOLESTEROL   5 MG.
SODIUM   113 MG.
DIETARY FIBER   8 G.

% CALORIES FROM:
PROTEIN: 19%
CARBOHYDRATE: 67%
FAT: 14%

FOOD EXCHANGES:
4 STARCH
4 VEGETABLE
1 FAT

MAKES 4 SERVINGS.

Enhance the rich, nutty flavor of plain almonds by toasting them on a shallow baking pan for 5 to 10 minutes at 350°.

> 15-ounce can black beans, rinsed and drained
> 14 1/2-ounce can no-added-salt stewed tomatoes, undrained
> 2 cups frozen mixed vegetables
> 1 cup water
> 3/4 cup uncooked brown rice
> 1/2 teaspoon thyme
> 1/2 teaspoon rosemary
> 1/8 teaspoon hot sauce
> 8-ounce can no-added-salt tomato sauce
> 1/3 cup slivered almonds, toasted
> 1/2 cup shredded low-fat mozzarella cheese

Combine beans, tomatoes, mixed vegetables, water, rice, spices, and hot sauce in a large skillet. Heat to boiling; reduce heat. Simmer, covered, for 12 to 14 minutes or until rice is tender. Stir in tomato sauce; heat through. Stir in toasted almonds. Sprinkle with shredded cheese, and serve.

Magic BEANS

Cheesy Bean Quiche

This quiche is a great meatless main dish; egg substitute keeps the cholesterol content low. Serve with a fruit salad and hot rolls for a complete meal.

Nonstick cooking spray

3/4 cup flour

1 1/2 cups shredded low-fat cheddar cheese

1 1/2 teaspoons baking powder

1/2 teaspoon salt

1/3 cup 2% milk

1/4 cup egg substitute, slightly beaten

16-ounce can garbanzo beans, rinsed and drained

16-ounce can kidney beans, rinsed and drained

8-ounce can no-added-salt tomato sauce

1/2 cup chopped red bell pepper

1/2 cup chopped green bell pepper

1 small onion, chopped

2 teaspoons chili powder

1/2 teaspoon oregano

1/2 teaspoon ground cumin

1/4 teaspoon garlic powder

Heat oven to 375°. Spray a pie plate with cooking spray. Mix flour, 1/2 cup of cheese, baking powder, and salt in a medium bowl. Stir in milk and egg substitute until blended. Spread over bottom and up side of pie plate. Mix 1/2 cup of the cheese with the remaining ingredients; spoon into pie plate. Bake uncovered about 25 minutes or until edge is puffy and light brown. Remove from oven; sprinkle with remaining 1/2 cup cheese. Let stand 10 minutes before cutting and serving.

PREPARATION TIME:
15 MINUTES

COOKING TIME:
25 MINUTES

STANDING TIME:
10 MINUTES

NUTRIENT INFORMATION
(PER SERVING):

SERVINGS PER RECIPE:	8
SERVING SIZE:	1/8 PIE
CALORIES	237
PROTEIN	15 G.
CARBOHYDRATE	33 G.
FAT	5 G.
SATURATED FAT	3 G.
CHOLESTEROL	16 MG.
SODIUM	396 MG.
DIETARY FIBER	7 G.

% CALORIES FROM:

PROTEIN:	25%
CARBOHYDRATE:	56%
FAT:	19%

FOOD EXCHANGES:
2 STARCH
1 MEDIUM-FAT MEAT
1 VEGETABLE

MAKES 8 SERVINGS.

Pam's Pita Tostadas

PREPARATION TIME:
15 MINUTES

NUTRIENT INFORMATION
(PER SERVING):
SERVINGS PER RECIPE: 4
SERVING SIZE: 1 TOSTADA
                  WITH TOPPINGS
CALORIES   427
PROTEIN   26 G.
CARBOHYDRATE   65 G.
FAT   7 G.
SATURATED FAT   3 G.
CHOLESTEROL   16 MG.
SODIUM   672 MG.
DIETARY FIBER   6 G.

% CALORIES FROM:
PROTEIN: 24%
CARBOHYDRATE: 61%
FAT: 15%

FOOD EXCHANGES:
4 STARCH
2 LEAN MEAT
1 VEGETABLE

MAKES 4 SERVINGS.

This is a quick and healthy alternative to the usual fat and calorie-laden Mexican foods. Garnish with fat-free sour cream or plain nonfat yogurt, and enjoy!

15-ounce can black beans, drained (reserve 3 tablespoons
    liquid), then rinsed
1 1/2 teaspoons ground cumin
4-ounce can diced green chiles
4 whole wheat pita breads
1/4 cup chopped red bell pepper
1/4 cup chopped green bell pepper
2 tablespoons chopped green onions
1/2 cup shredded low-fat cheddar cheese
1/2 cup shredded low-fat Monterey Jack cheese
1/2 cup shredded lettuce
1/4 cup chopped fresh cilantro
1/2 cup medium salsa

Place beans, reserved liquid, cumin, and chiles in a blender or food processor. Blend until smooth. Spread bean mixture on pita breads. Top with bell peppers, onions, cheese, lettuce, and cilantro. Serve with salsa.

Magic BEANS

Lentil One-Dish Dinner

This satisfying dish takes only minutes to assemble.

1 cup lentils, uncooked and rinsed

1/2 cup uncooked brown rice

2 cups sliced carrots

3 cups water

1 packet onion soup mix

1 teaspoon garlic powder

1 teaspoon basil

1 tablespoon olive oil

Place all ingredients in a large pot. Bring to a boil. Reduce heat, cover, and cook until rice is done, 20 to 30 minutes.

PREPARATION TIME:
5 MINUTES

COOKING TIME:
30 MINUTES

NUTRIENT INFORMATION
(PER SERVING):

SERVINGS PER RECIPE:	4
SERVING SIZE:	1 1/2 CUPS
CALORIES	317
PROTEIN	12 G.
CARBOHYDRATE	56 G.
FAT	5 G.
SATURATED FAT	1 G.
CHOLESTEROL	<1 MG.
SODIUM	258 MG.
DIETARY FIBER	5 G.

% CALORIES FROM:

PROTEIN:	15%
CARBOHYDRATE:	71%
FAT:	14%

FOOD EXCHANGES:
3 STARCH
2 VEGETABLE
1 FAT

MAKES 4 SERVINGS.

Mediterranean Pocket Sandwiches

PREPARATION TIME:
10 MINUTES

COOKING TIME:
4 MINUTES

NUTRIENT INFORMATION
(PER SERVING):

SERVINGS PER RECIPE:	8
SERVING SIZE: 1/2 PITA POCKET	
WITH FILLING	
CALORIES	192
PROTEIN	9 G.
CARBOHYDRATE	30 G.
FAT	4 G.
SATURATED FAT	1 G.
CHOLESTEROL	2 MG.
SODIUM	319 MG.
DIETARY FIBER	3 G.

% CALORIES FROM:

PROTEIN:	19%
CARBOHYDRATE:	62%
FAT:	19%

FOOD EXCHANGES:
2 STARCH
1 LEAN MEAT

MAKES 8 SERVINGS.

Using the microwave and food processor cuts the preparation time for this healthy lunchtime sandwich.

1/2 cup chopped green onions

1/2 cup chopped red bell pepper

1/2 cup chopped green bell pepper

3 tablespoons chopped fresh parsley

1 tablespoon celery seeds

1 tablespoon diet margarine

1/2 teaspoon oregano

1/2 teaspoon mint flakes

1/2 teaspoon garlic powder

1/8 teaspoon cayenne pepper

15-ounce can garbanzo beans, rinsed and drained

4 whole wheat pita bread rounds, halved and opened into pockets

1/2 cup shredded low-fat Monterey Jack cheese

1 medium tomato, cut into 8 slices

2 cups alfalfa sprouts

Combine green onions, peppers, parsley, celery seeds, margarine, oregano, mint, garlic powder, and cayenne pepper in a 1-quart casserole. Cover with vented plastic wrap, and microwave on high for 3 minutes. Place onion mixture and garbanzo beans in a blender or food processor. Process 1 minute or until smooth. Spoon about 1/4 cup bean mixture into each pita bread half; top with 1 tablespoon cheese. Cover with paper towels, and microwave on high for 1 minute. Cut tomato slices in half. Place 2 tomato slice halves and 1/4 cup alfalfa sprouts into each sandwich half. Serve immediately.

 Magic BEANS

Turkey Taco-Tico

Children enjoy the fun of make-your-own tacos. Serve rice or fruit salad on the side to budding young chefs.

1 teaspoon olive oil

1 pound ground turkey

1 cup chopped onions

1/2 cup chopped green bell pepper

1/2 cup chopped red bell pepper

1 clove garlic, minced

1 tablespoon chili powder

1 teaspoon oregano

1/2 teaspoon ground cumin

15-ounce can kidney beans, rinsed and drained

1 cup no-salt-added tomato sauce

8 flour tortillas

1 cup shredded lettuce

1 cup diced tomato

1/2 cup shredded low-fat cheddar cheese

1/2 cup shredded low-fat Monterey Jack cheese

1 cup medium salsa

1 cup fat-free sour cream

Heat oil in a large nonstick pan over medium heat. Add the turkey, and sauté for a few minutes. Add onions, peppers, garlic, and spices. Continue to sauté until turkey is thoroughly brown, then drain off any fat. Add the beans and tomato sauce, and simmer for 20 minutes. Scoop the turkey mixture onto tortillas, and top with lettuce, tomato, cheese, salsa, and sour cream. Fold tortillas around filling.

PREPARATION TIME:
15 MINUTES

COOKING TIME:
30 MINUTES

NUTRIENT INFORMATION
(PER SERVING):
SERVINGS PER RECIPE: 8
SERVING SIZE: 1 TORTILLA
WITH TOPPINGS

CALORIES	335
PROTEIN	22 G.
CARBOHYDRATE	37 G.
FAT	11 G.
SATURATED FAT	3 G.
CHOLESTEROL	56 MG.
SODIUM	538 MG.
DIETARY FIBER	5 G.

% CALORIES FROM:

PROTEIN:	26%
CARBOHYDRATE:	44%
FAT:	30%

FOOD EXCHANGES:
2 STARCH
2 MEDIUM-FAT MEAT
1 VEGETABLE

MAKES 8 SERVINGS.

Vegetarian Tortillas

PREPARATION TIME:
5 MINUTES

COOKING TIME:
6 MINUTES

NUTRIENT INFORMATION
(PER SERVING):
SERVINGS PER RECIPE: 4
SERVING SIZE: 2 TORTILLAS
                WITH FILLING
CALORIES   392
PROTEIN   18 G.
CARBOHYDRATE   62 G.
FAT   8 G.
SATURATED FAT   2 G.
CHOLESTEROL   6 MG.
SODIUM   968 MG.
DIETARY FIBER   6 G.

% CALORIES FROM:
PROTEIN: 18%
CARBOHYDRATE: 63%
FAT: 18%

FOOD EXCHANGES:
4 STARCH
1 LEAN MEAT
1 FAT

MAKES 4 SERVINGS.

Using the microwave cuts preparation time so the family can enjoy this delicious main dish in a hurry!

16-ounce can fat-free refried beans
1/2 cup mild salsa
1/2 teaspoon chili powder
1/2 teaspoon ground cumin
8 flour tortillas
1 cup shredded lettuce
1/2 cup shredded low-fat Monterey Jack cheese

Mix beans, salsa, chili powder, and cumin in a 2-quart saucepan. Heat over medium heat about 5 minutes, stirring occasionally, until warm. Wrap tortillas in damp paper towels, and microwave on high 15 to 20 seconds or until warm. Place bean mixture in the center of each tortilla; spread slightly. Top each tortilla with lettuce and cheese. Fold tortilla around filling.

Magic BEANS

Mexibean Lasagna

This dish tastes great on the second day—if you're lucky enough to have any leftovers!

2 teaspoons olive oil

1 cup chopped onion

2 cloves garlic, minced

1 green pepper, coarsely chopped

1 teaspoon ground cumin

2 teaspoons chili powder

1/8 teaspoon cayenne pepper

1 cup frozen or fresh corn kernels

15-ounce can dark red kidney beans, rinsed and drained

1 cup no-added-salt tomato sauce

4-ounce can diced green chiles, drained

Nonstick cooking spray

6 corn tortillas

1 cup fat-free cottage cheese

3/4 cup shredded low-fat cheddar cheese

In a large skillet, heat oil over medium-high heat. Sauté onion, garlic, and green pepper for about 5 minutes or until soft. Stir in spices, and sauté 1 additional minute. Remove from heat. Mix in corn, beans, tomato sauce, and diced green chiles. Spray a 13" x 9" dish with cooking spray. Place 3 tortillas in the dish, arranging to cover the bottom. Spoon in half of the corn mixture, and spread 1/2 cup cottage cheese on top. Sprinkle with half of the cheddar cheese. Repeat layers, using up all the ingredients. Cook, uncovered at 350° for 45 minutes, until casserole is heated through and cheddar cheese has melted. Let stand 5 minutes before serving.

PREPARATION TIME:
15 MINUTES

COOKING TIME:
50 MINUTES

STANDING TIME:
5 MINUTES

NUTRIENT INFORMATION (PER SERVING):

SERVINGS PER RECIPE:	6
SERVING SIZE:	1 1/2 CUPS
CALORIES	298
PROTEIN	21 G.
CARBOHYDRATE	40 G.
FAT	6 G.
SATURATED FAT	<1 G.
CHOLESTEROL	12 MG.
SODIUM	320 MG.
DIETARY FIBER	6 G.

% CALORIES FROM:

PROTEIN:	28%
CARBOHYDRATE:	54%
FAT:	18%

FOOD EXCHANGES:
2 STARCH
1 LEAN MEAT
2 VEGETABLE

MAKES 6 SERVINGS.

Robust Beans and Rice

PREPARATION TIME:
10 MINUTES

COOKING TIME:
85 MINUTES

NUTRIENT INFORMATION
(PER SERVING):
SERVINGS PER RECIPE: 7
SERVING SIZE: 1 CUP
CALORIES   339
PROTEIN   20 G.
CARBOHYDRATE   40 G.
FAT   11 G.
SATURATED FAT   5 G.
CHOLESTEROL   43 MG.
SODIUM   341 MG.
DIETARY FIBER   6 G.

% CALORIES FROM:
PROTEIN: 24%
CARBOHYDRATE: 47%
FAT: 29%

FOOD EXCHANGES:
2 STARCH
1 MEDIUM-FAT MEAT
2 VEGETABLE
1 FAT

MAKES 7 SERVINGS.

This hearty dish takes only minutes to put together. Let your oven do the work while you prepare a fruit salad as an accompaniment.

>   1 pound extra lean ground beef
>   1/2 cup chopped onion
>   1 cup long grain rice, uncooked
>   7 ounces water
>   3/4 teaspoon chili powder
>   1/2 teaspoon ground cumin
>   1/4 teaspoon cayenne pepper
>   15-ounce can pinto beans, rinsed and drained
>   11 1/2-ounce can tomato juice
>   4-ounce can diced green chiles, undrained
>   Nonstick cooking spray

Cook meat and onion in a large nonstick skillet over medium heat until meat is browned, stirring to crumble. Drain meat mixture into a colander, and pat dry with paper towels. Combine meat mixture with the next 8 ingredients, and stir well. Pour mixture into a 3-quart casserole coated with cooking spray. Cover and bake at 350° for 50 minutes. Stir. Cover and bake an additional 30 minutes or until rice is tender.

Magic BEANS

Rush Hour Chicken

This is a quick and delicious one-dish meal—perfect for busy days!

- 3/4 pound boneless, skinless chicken breast, cut into thin strips
- 2 teaspoons olive oil
- 16-ounce can black beans, rinsed and drained
- 16-ounce package seasoned frozen vegetables and pasta
- 3/4 cup chunky salsa
- 1 tablespoon chopped fresh cilantro

In a large skillet, brown chicken breast in oil. Stir in black beans, vegetables and pasta, and salsa. Cover; simmer 10 minutes until vegetables are crisp-tender, stirring occasionally. Sprinkle with cilantro.

PREPARATION TIME:
10 MINUTES

COOKING TIME:
15 MINUTES

NUTRIENT INFORMATION
(PER SERVING):

SERVINGS PER RECIPE:	6
SERVING SIZE:	1/2 CUPS
CALORIES	95
PROTEIN	27 G.
CARBOHYDRATE	31G.
FAT	7 G.
SATURATED FAT	3 G.
CHOLESTEROL	54 MG.
SODIUM	479 MG.
DIETARY FIBER	5 G.

% CALORIES FROM:

PROTEIN:	37%
CARBOHYDRATE:	42%
FAT:	21%

FOOD EXCHANGES:
2 STARCH
3 VERY LEAN MEAT
1 FAT

MAKES 6 SERVINGS.

Black Bean Pizza

PREPARATION TIME:
20 MINUTES

COOKING TIME:
17 MINUTES

NUTRIENT INFORMATION
(PER SERVING):

SERVINGS PER RECIPE:	3
SERVING SIZE:	1 PIZZA
CALORIES	480
PROTEIN	45 G.
CARBOHYDRATE	57 G.
FAT	8 G.
SATURATED FAT	2 G.
CHOLESTEROL	59 MG.
SODIUM	435 MG.
DIETARY FIBER	7 G.

% CALORIES FROM:

PROTEIN:	38%
CARBOHYDRATE:	48%
FAT:	15%

FOOD EXCHANGES:
4 STARCH
4 VERY LEAN MEAT
1 FAT

MAKES 3 SERVINGS.

Try this unusual variation of an old Italian favorite.

Nonstick cooking spray

2 teaspoons cornmeal

1 loaf frozen white bread dough, thawed

2 boneless, skinless chicken breast halves, shredded or cut into 1/2-inch cubes

1/2 teaspoon cumin

16-ounce can black beans, rinsed and drained

1/2 cup picante sauce

1 medium green pepper, chopped

1 medium tomato, chopped

1 cup sliced mushrooms

3 tablespoons chopped fresh cilantro

3/4 cup shredded low-fat Monterey Jack cheese

Preheat oven to 450°. Lightly coat three pizza pans with cooking spray. Cover pans with an even sprinkling of cornmeal. Divide dough into three equal portions, then roll each portion into a 7-inch circle. Place dough on coated pizza pans. Prick crust with fork, then bake at 450° for 8 minutes.

While dough is baking, spray a medium nonstick skillet with cooking spray. Heat over medium heat until hot. Add chicken and cumin; cook and stir until chicken is no longer pink. Remove from heat. Stir in beans and picante sauce. Mix well.

Spread bean and chicken mixture evenly over partially baked crusts. Cover with green pepper, tomato, and mushrooms. Sprinkle with cilantro and cheese, then bake at 450° for 7 to 9 minutes or until cheese is melted and crusts are golden brown.

Magic BEANS

Pork Chops With Salsa Beans and Rice

Salsa adds punch to pork with beans and rice. Choose mild, medium, or hot salsa, depending on your taste.

1 tablespoon olive oil

5 pork chops, about 1/4-inch thick

2 14 1/2-ounce cans no-added-salt stewed tomatoes, undrained

16-ounce can red kidney beans, rinsed and drained

4-ounce can diced green chiles, drained

1 cup uncooked brown rice

1 cup low-sodium chicken broth

1 teaspoon ground cumin

1/2 teaspoon cilantro

1/2 cup medium salsa

1/2 cup shredded low-fat cheddar cheese

2 tablespoons chopped green onions

Heat oven to 350°. Brown pork chops in oil in a medium skillet; remove from skillet, and drain. Mix tomatoes, beans, green chiles, rice, broth, cumin, and cilantro in the same skillet. Heat to boiling; remove from heat. Spoon mixture into an ungreased 13" x 9" pan. Place pork chops on the mixture. Cover and bake about 45 minutes or until pork is tender. Spoon salsa over pork. Sprinkle with cheese. Bake uncovered 1 to 2 minutes or until cheese is melted. Sprinkle with onions before serving.

PREPARATION TIME:
10 MINUTES

COOKING TIME:
55 MINUTES

NUTRIENT INFORMATION
(PER SERVING):

SERVINGS PER RECIPE:	5
SERVING SIZE:	1 PORK CHOP WITH 1/2 CUP RICE MIXTURE
CALORIES	440
PROTEIN	36 G.
CARBOHYDRATE	47 G.
FAT	12 G.
SATURATED FAT	4 G.
CHOLESTEROL	73 MG.
SODIUM	269 MG.
DIETARY FIBER	6 G.

% CALORIES FROM:

PROTEIN:	33%
CARBOHYDRATE:	43%
FAT:	24%

FOOD EXCHANGES:
2 STARCH
4 LEAN MEAT
3 VEGETABLE

MAKES 5 SERVINGS.

Spanish One-Dish Dinner

PREPARATION TIME:
10 MINUTES

COOKING TIME:
40 MINUTES

NUTRIENT INFORMATION
(PER SERVING):
SERVINGS PER RECIPE: 6
SERVING SIZE: 1 1/2 CUPS
CALORIES   331
PROTEIN   14 G.
CARBOHYDRATE   44 G.
FAT   11 G.
SATURATED FAT   4 G.
CHOLESTEROL   38 MG.
SODIUM   388 MG.
DIETARY FIBER   4 G.

% CALORIES FROM:
PROTEIN: 17%
CARBOHYDRATE: 53%
FAT: 30%

FOOD EXCHANGES:
2 STARCH
1 MEDIUM-FAT MEAT
1 FRUIT
1 FAT

MAKES 6 SERVINGS.

One-dish dinners save time, both in preparation and cleanup. This recipe makes a complete meal when served with a crispy green salad on the side.

3/4 pound extra lean ground beef
Nonstick cooking spray
1/2 cup chopped onion
2 cloves garlic, minced
14 1/2-ounce can no-added-salt whole tomatoes, undrained and chopped
4-ounce can diced green chiles, drained
1/3 cup raisins
1/2 teaspoon salt
1/2 teaspoon pepper
1/2 teaspoon cinnamon
1/4 teaspoon cloves
1/4 teaspoon allspice
1/4 teaspoon nutmeg
1/4 teaspoon grated orange rind
1/8 teaspoon hot sauce
1 cup canned black beans, rinsed and drained
2 cups peeled, finely chopped cooking apple
3 cups hot cooked rice

Cook meat in a skillet over medium heat until browned, stirring to crumble. Drain in a colander; pat dry with paper towels, and set aside. Wipe drippings from skillet with paper towel. Coat skillet with cooking spray; place over medium heat until hot. Add onion and garlic; sauté 2 minutes or until tender. Return meat to skillet. Add tomatoes, green chiles, raisins, salt, pepper, spices, orange rind, and hot sauce. Bring to a boil, then reduce heat, and simmer, uncovered, 15 minutes. Add beans and apple. Cook 10 minutes or until heated, stirring occasionally. Serve over rice.

Magic BEANS

Turkey-Bean Tater Topper

Spice up a plain potato with this savory, high-fiber topping. To make baked potatoes in a flash, use the microwave: Wash potatoes, and pierce skin with a fork in several places. Wrap each potato in a paper towel, and arrange in a circle in the microwave. Cook on high for 5 minutes, then turn potatoes and cook an additional 5 minutes.

2 teaspoons olive oil

1 pound turkey tenderloins, cut into 1-inch strips

1/4 teaspoon garlic powder

1/2 cup chopped onions

1 clove garlic, minced

1/2 cup chopped red bell pepper

1/2 cup chopped green bell pepper

1 1/2 cups tomato juice

1/2 cup canned black beans, rinsed and drained

1/2 cup canned navy beans, rinsed and drained

1/2 teaspoon chili powder

1/4 teaspoon ground cumin

1/2 teaspoon oregano

1/2 teaspoon cilantro

4 large potatoes, baked

Heat olive oil in a large nonstick skillet. Add turkey, and sprinkle with garlic powder. Cook, stirring frequently, until tenderloins are cooked through (4 to 6 minutes). Transfer them to a plate with a slotted spoon. Add onions, garlic, and peppers to the skillet. Cook, stirring frequently, until the vegetables are tender, 2 to 3 minutes. Stir in the juice, beans, chili powder, cumin, oregano, and cilantro. Simmer 8 to 10 minutes until the bean mixture is thick. Return the turkey tenderloins to the skillet, and cook an additional 2 minutes until the bean mixture is hot. Cut open the hot potatoes, and top them with the bean mixture.

PREPARATION TIME:
15 MINUTES

COOKING TIME:
20 MINUTES

NUTRIENT INFORMATION
(PER SERVING):
SERVINGS PER RECIPE: 4
SERVING SIZE: 1 BAKED POTATO
                        WITH TOPPING
CALORIES   572
PROTEIN   43 G.
CARBOHYDRATE   73 G.
FAT   12 G.
SATURATED FAT   3 G.
CHOLESTEROL   86 MG.
SODIUM   400 MG.
DIETARY FIBER   10 G.

% CALORIES FROM:
PROTEIN: 30%
CARBOHYDRATE: 51%
FAT: 19%

FOOD EXCHANGES:
4 STARCH
4 LEAN MEAT
2 VEGETABLE

MAKES 4 SERVINGS.

Vegetable Bean Tostadas

PREPARATION TIME:
15 MINUTES

COOKING TIME:
15 MINUTES

NUTRIENT INFORMATION
(PER SERVING):
SERVINGS PER RECIPE: 6
SERVING SIZE: 1 TORTILLA
                WITH TOPPINGS
CALORIES   245
PROTEIN   11 G.
CARBOHYDRATE   39 G.
FAT   5 G.
SATURATED FAT   1 G.
CHOLESTEROL   1 MG.
SODIUM   466 MG.
DIETARY FIBER   5 G.

% CALORIES FROM:
PROTEIN: 18%
CARBOHYDRATE: 64%
FAT: 18%

FOOD EXCHANGES:
2 STARCH
2 VEGETABLE
1 FAT

MAKES 6 SERVINGS.

Serve with a citrus salad for a complete vegetarian meal. The bean mixture also makes a nice dip for baked tortilla chips.

6 flour tortillas
1/3 cup fat-free cottage cheese
1/4 teaspoon salt
2 tablespoons lemon juice
15-ounce can garbanzo beans, rinsed and drained
Nonstick cooking spray
1/4 cup minced onion
1 clove garlic, minced
1/4 cup chopped fresh parsley
1 teaspoon fresh cilantro
1 tablespoon sesame seeds, toasted
2 cups thinly sliced cucumber
3 cups shredded fresh spinach
3 cups chopped tomato
6 tablespoons fat-free sour cream
1 tablespoon finely chopped green onions

Arrange tortillas in a single layer on a baking sheet. Bake at 350° for 6 minutes on each side until crisp. Let cool on a wire rack. Place cottage cheese, salt, lemon juice, and garbanzo beans in a blender or food processor; process until smooth. Spoon mixture into a bowl; set aside. Coat a small nonstick skillet with cooking spray. Place over medium-high heat until hot. Add onion and garlic; sauté 2 minutes or until tender. Add the onion mixture, parsley, cilantro, and sesame seeds to bean mixture; stir well.

To serve: spread bean mixture evenly over each tortilla. Top with cucumber, spinach, tomato, sour cream, and green onions.

Magic BEANS

BAKED BEANS
& BEYOND
*Side
Dishes*

Speedy Spicy Beans and Rice

This made-in-minutes side dish is a wonderful accompaniment for a Mexican meal.

16-ounce can kidney beans, undrained
1 cup water
3/4 cup picante sauce
1 1/2 cups uncooked quick-cooking rice
1 tablespoon parsley

Bring kidney beans, water, and picante sauce to a boil in a medium saucepan. Stir in rice; cover. Remove from heat. Let stand 5 minutes. Fluff with fork. Sprinkle with parsley to garnish.

PREPARATION TIME:
5 MINUTES

STANDING TIME:
5 MINUTES

NUTRIENT INFORMATION
(PER SERVING):

SERVINGS PER RECIPE:	8
SERVING SIZE:	1/2 CUP
CALORIES	189
PROTEIN	6 G.
CARBOHYDRATE	39 G.
FAT	<1 G.
SATURATED FAT	<1 G.
CHOLESTEROL	<1 MG.
SODIUM	352 MG.
DIETARY FIBER	3 G.

% CALORIES FROM:

PROTEIN:	13%
CARBOHYDRATE:	83%
FAT:	4%

FOOD EXCHANGES:
2 STARCH
1 VEGETABLE

MAKES 8 SERVINGS.

Olga's Garden Vegetables and Beans

PREPARATION TIME:
20 MINUTES

COOKING TIME:
20 MINUTES

NUTRIENT INFORMATION
(PER SERVING):
SERVINGS PER RECIPE: 12
SERVING SIZE: 1/2 CUP
CALORIES   154
PROTEIN   8 G.
CARBOHYDRATE   26 G.
FAT   2 G.
SATURATED FAT   <1 G.
CHOLESTEROL   0 MG.
SODIUM   102 MG.
DIETARY FIBER   4 G.

% CALORIES FROM:
PROTEIN: 21%
CARBOHYDRATE: 68%
FAT: 11%

FOOD EXCHANGES:
2 STARCH

MAKES 12 SERVINGS.

Garden-fresh vegetables and a nice blend of spices enhance this side dish. Increase portion sizes and serve over cooked rice for a meatless main dish.

1 tablespoon canola oil
1/4 cup chopped green onions
1/2 teaspoon ginger
2 cloves garlic, minced
1/4 cup low-sodium chicken broth
1 teaspoon curry powder
1/2 teaspoon salt
1/8 teaspoon cayenne pepper
1/2 teaspoon parsley
2 small zucchini, chopped
1 small eggplant, cut into 1-inch pieces
1 red bell pepper, thinly sliced
1 green bell pepper, thinly sliced
2 15-ounce cans cannellini beans, rinsed and drained

Heat oil in a large skillet over medium high heat. Cook onions, ginger, and garlic in oil until onions are crisp-tender, about 2 minutes, stirring occasionally. Stir in remaining ingredients except cannellini beans. Cook about 5 minutes, stirring frequently, until vegetables are crisp-tender. Stir in beans; heat through.

Magic BEANS

Tex-Mex Baked Beans

South-of-the-border taste in spicy baked beans!

1 tablespoon olive oil
1 medium onion, chopped
1 red bell pepper, chopped
1 green bell pepper, chopped
16-ounce can navy beans, rinsed and drained
16-ounce can kidney beans, rinsed and drained
16-ounce can pinto beans, rinsed and drained
16-ounce can no-added-salt stewed tomatoes
1 teaspoon oregano
1/2 teaspoon ground cumin
1/2 teaspoon black pepper
1/4 teaspoon cayenne pepper
Nonstick cooking spray

Heat oil in a skillet over medium-high heat until hot. Add onion and peppers; sauté until tender. Combine beans, tomatoes, oregano, cumin, and peppers in a 3-quart casserole coated with cooking spray. Cover and bake for 1 hour.

PREPARATION TIME:
10 MINUTES

COOKING TIME:
60 MINUTES

NUTRIENT INFORMATION
(PER SERVING):
SERVINGS PER RECIPE: 8
SERVING SIZE: 1 CUP
CALORIES   279
PROTEIN   14 G.
CARBOHYDRATE   49 G.
FAT   3 G.
SATURATED FAT   <1 G.
CHOLESTEROL   0 MG.
SODIUM   125 MG.
DIETARY FIBER   12 G.

% CALORIES FROM:
PROTEIN: 20%
CARBOHYDRATE: 70%
FAT: 10%

FOOD EXCHANGES:
3 STARCH
1 LEAN MEAT
1 VEGETABLE

MAKES 8 SERVINGS.

Confetti Black Beans and Rice

PREPARATION TIME:
10 MINUTES

COOKING TIME:
30 MINUTES

NUTRIENT INFORMATION
(PER SERVING):

SERVINGS PER RECIPE: 6
SERVING SIZE: 1 CUP
CALORIES   245
PROTEIN   9 G.
CARBOHYDRATE   41 G.
FAT   5 G.
SATURATED FAT   1 G.
CHOLESTEROL   0 MG.
SODIUM   225 MG.
DIETARY FIBER   4 G.

% CALORIES FROM:
PROTEIN: 15%
CARBOHYDRATE: 67%
FAT: 18%

FOOD EXCHANGES:
2 STARCH
2 VEGETABLE
1 FAT

MAKES 6 SERVINGS.

This side dish perks up any plate.

15-ounce can low-sodium chicken broth
5-ounce package yellow rice mix
2 tablespoons olive oil
1 yellow onion, minced
2 cloves garlic, minced
1/2 yellow pepper, chopped
1/2 green pepper, chopped
1/2 red pepper, chopped
15-ounce can black beans, rinsed and drained
1 tomato, diced
1/2 teaspoon black pepper
1/2 teaspoon garlic powder
1/2 teaspoon onion powder

In a medium saucepan, bring chicken broth to a boil. Add rice mix, and simmer on low, covered, for 20 minutes. Meanwhile, heat olive oil in a skillet, and sauté onion, garlic, and peppers until soft (about 3 to 4 minutes). Drain excess liquid. Add beans and tomato to sautéed vegetables, and heat thoroughly. Season with pepper, garlic, and onion powder. Mix bean mixture with yellow rice, and serve.

 Magic BEANS

Black-Eyed Peas on the Side

This makes a great side dish or it can be served in a large portion for a main dish.

4 slices bacon, cut into 1-inch pieces

2 1/2 cups low-sodium chicken broth

1 cup dried black-eyed peas, rinsed

2 medium stalks celery, sliced

1 large onion, chopped

1 1/2 teaspoons savory

1/4 teaspoon cayenne pepper

1 clove garlic, minced

3 medium carrots, thinly sliced

1 green bell pepper, cut into 1-inch pieces

1 red bell pepper, cut into 1-inch pieces

1/2 cup low-fat shredded Monterey Jack cheese

Cook bacon in a medium skillet until crisp. Remove bacon, blot with paper towels, and set aside. Drain fat from skillet. Heat broth, black-eyed peas, celery, onion, savory, cayenne pepper, and garlic to boiling in the same skillet. Boil uncovered 2 minutes; reduce heat. Cover and simmer about 40 minutes, stirring occasionally, until peas are almost tender. Stir in carrots and peppers. Heat to simmering. Cover and simmer about 15 minutes, stirring occasionally, until vegetables are tender. Sprinkle with cheese and crumbled bacon.

PREPARATION TIME:
10 MINUTES

COOKING TIME:
65 MINUTES

NUTRIENT INFORMATION
(PER SERVING):

SERVINGS PER RECIPE:	6
SERVING SIZE:	3/4 CUP
CALORIES	233
PROTEIN	14 G.
CARBOHYDRATE	33 G.
FAT	5 G.
SATURATED FAT	1 G.
CHOLESTEROL	7 MG.
SODIUM	157 MG.
DIETARY FIBER	3 G.

% CALORIES FROM:

PROTEIN:	24%
CARBOHYDRATE:	57%
FAT:	19%

FOOD EXCHANGES:
2 STARCH
1 LEAN MEAT

MAKES 6 SERVINGS.

Black Bean, Pasta, and Artichoke Heart Medley

PREPARATION TIME:
10 MINUTES

COOKING TIME:
25 MINUTES

NUTRIENT INFORMATION
(PER SERVING):

SERVINGS PER RECIPE:	12
SERVING SIZE:	3/4 CUP
CALORIES	154
PROTEIN	7 G.
CARBOHYDRATE	29 G.
FAT	2 G.
SATURATED FAT	<1 G.
CHOLESTEROL	0 MG.
SODIUM	89 MG.
DIETARY FIBER	4 G.

% CALORIES FROM:

PROTEIN:	17%
CARBOHYDRATE:	72%
FAT:	11%

FOOD EXCHANGES:
2 STARCH

MAKES 12 SERVINGS.

Black beans are becoming more popular in the United States, although they have been a staple of South American cuisine for centuries. Their mushroom-like flavor mixes well with pasta and artichoke hearts in this side dish.

1 tablespoon olive oil
1 cup sliced green onions
1/2 teaspoon oregano
1/2 teaspoon basil
1/4 teaspoon salt
1/8 teaspoon black pepper
1/8 teaspoon cayenne pepper
1 clove garlic, minced
2 14 1/2-ounce cans no-added-salt whole tomatoes,
    undrained and chopped
15-ounce can black beans, rinsed and drained
4 cups hot cooked pasta (choose any shape)
14-ounce can artichoke hearts, drained and quartered

Heat oil in a large nonstick skillet over medium heat. Add green onions, and sauté 5 minutes. Add oregano, basil, salt, peppers, garlic, and tomatoes; cover and simmer 10 minutes. Add beans; cover and simmer an additional 5 minutes. Combine bean mixture, hot cooked pasta, and artichoke hearts in a large bowl. Toss well. Serve warm or at room temperature.

Magic BEANS

Curried Lentils With Fruit

This side dish is especially suited for pork entrees. Lentils are an excellent base for the sweet taste of apples, raisins, and curry.

1 1/2 cups lentils, uncooked

2 quarts water

1 yellow apple, cored, peeled, and chopped

1/4 cup golden raisins

1/4 cup nonfat lemon yogurt

1 teaspoon curry powder

1/2 teaspoon salt

Combine lentils and water in a large saucepan. Bring to a boil over high heat. Reduce heat and simmer 20 minutes, stirring occasionally. Stir apple and raisins into saucepan; cook 10 minutes or until lentils are tender. Drain well. Place lentil mixture in large serving bowl. Stir in yogurt, curry powder, and salt until well blended.

PREPARATION TIME:
10 MINUTES

COOKING TIME:
30 MINUTES

NUTRIENT INFORMATION
(PER SERVING):

SERVINGS PER RECIPE:	6
SERVING SIZE:	1/2 CUP
CALORIES	141
PROTEIN	6 G.
CARBOHYDRATE	28 G.
FAT	<1 G.
SATURATED FAT	<1 G.
CHOLESTEROL	<1 MG.
SODIUM	299 MG.
DIETARY FIBER	2 G.

% CALORIES FROM:

PROTEIN:	17%
CARBOHYDRATE:	79%
FAT:	4%

FOOD EXCHANGES:
2 STARCH

MAKES 6 SERVINGS.

Bang-Up Boston Baked Beans

PREPARATION TIME:
20 MINUTES

COOKING TIME:
1 HOUR

NUTRIENT INFORMATION
(PER SERVING):
SERVINGS PER RECIPE: 10
SERVING SIZE: 3/4 CUP
CALORIES   234
PROTEIN   9 G.
CARBOHYDRATE   45 G.
FAT   2 G.
SATURATED FAT   1 G.
CHOLESTEROL   3 MG.
SODIUM   299 MG.
DIETARY FIBER   6 G.

% CALORIES FROM:
PROTEIN: 15%
CARBOHYDRATE: 77%
FAT: 8%

FOOD EXCHANGES:
3 STARCH

MAKES 10 SERVINGS.

"And this is good old Boston, the home of the bean and the cod, where the Lowells talk only to Cabots and the Cabots talk only to God." (John Collins Bossidy) This is an updated version of a classic bean dish—now low in fat, yet still rich in flavor.

Nonstick cooking spray
2 cups minced onion
1 cup chopped green bell pepper
2 15-ounce cans navy beans, rinsed and drained
1/2 cup molasses
1/3 cup ketchup
1/4 cup firmly packed brown sugar
2 tablespoons prepared mustard
1 teaspoon paprika
1/2 teaspoon salt
1/4 teaspoon pepper
1/8 teaspoon cayenne pepper
5 slices raw bacon, chopped

Coat a skillet with cooking spray, and heat over medium high heat until hot. Add onion and bell pepper, and sauté for 5 minutes or until tender. In a 1 1/2-quart casserole coated with cooking spray, combine onions and pepper with remaining ingredients. Stir to blend. Cover and bake at 350° for 30 minutes. Uncover and bake an additional 30 minutes or until sauce thickens.

Magic BEANS

Lucky 13 Marinated Beans

Prepared bean soup mix adds variety to this chilled side dish. Make this dish the night before you need it; cooking the dried beans takes some time, but the flavor is worth it!

12-ounce package 13-bean soup mix

2 quarts water

2/3 cup fat-free Italian salad dressing

1 tablespoon red wine vinegar

1/2 teaspoon dried Italian seasoning

1/8 teaspoon crushed red pepper

1/8 teaspoon black pepper

1 1/2 cups cherry tomatoes, quartered

1/2 cup sliced green onions

Rinse beans; place in a Dutch oven. Add water and bring to a boil. Reduce heat, and simmer 80 minutes or until beans are tender. Drain. Combine Italian dressing, vinegar, Italian seasoning, and peppers; pour over beans, and toss gently. Cover and chill at least 8 hours, stirring occasionally. Just before serving, add tomatoes and green onions to bean mixture. Toss gently and serve.

PREPARATION TIME:
10 MINUTES

COOKING TIME:
80 MINUTES

CHILLING TIME:
8 HOURS

NUTRIENT INFORMATION
(PER SERVING):

SERVINGS PER RECIPE:	12
SERVING SIZE:	1/2 CUP
CALORIES	109
PROTEIN	6 G.
CARBOHYDRATE	19 G.
FAT	1 G.
SATURATED FAT	<1 G.
CHOLESTEROL	0 MG.
SODIUM	148 MG.
DIETARY FIBER	1 G.

% CALORIES FROM:

PROTEIN:	22%
CARBOHYDRATE:	70%
FAT:	8%

FOOD EXCHANGES:
1 STARCH
1 VEGETABLE

MAKES 12 SERVINGS.

Citrus Cannellini

PREPARATION TIME:
5 MINUTES

COOKING TIME:
10 MINUTES

NUTRIENT INFORMATION
(PER SERVING):
SERVINGS PER RECIPE: 8
SERVING SIZE: 3/4 CUP
CALORIES   261
PROTEIN   10 G.
CARBOHYDRATE   53 G.
FAT   1 G.
SATURATED FAT   <1 G.
CHOLESTEROL   0 MG.
SODIUM   394 MG.
DIETARY FIBER   7 G.

% CALORIES FROM:
PROTEIN: 15%
CARBOHYDRATE: 81%
FAT: 3%

FOOD EXCHANGES:
3 STARCH
1 VEGETABLE

MAKES 8 SERVINGS.

This side dish has a surprisingly fresh and delicate flavor, which makes it a nice accompaniment to many grilled entrees.

2 15-ounce cans cannellini beans, rinsed and drained
1 medium onion, chopped
1/2 cup orange marmalade
1/3 cup firmly packed brown sugar
1 tablespoon Dijon mustard
1/2 teaspoon rosemary
1/4 teaspoon salt
1/4 teaspoon black pepper

In a large saucepan, combine all ingredients and mix thoroughly. Simmer over medium heat for 10 minutes or until heated through.

 Magic BEANS

Red and White Pasta, Tomatoes, and Beans

This simple side dish is a good source of fiber. Increase the portion size and it doubles as a meatless main dish.

8 ounces small shell pasta, uncooked

1 tablespoon olive oil

1 small onion, chopped

1 clove garlic, minced

15-ounce can cannellini beans, rinsed and drained

1 cup low-sodium chicken broth

1 teaspoon sage

1 teaspoon oregano

1/2 teaspoon basil

1/4 teaspoon salt

1/8 teaspoon pepper

1 1/2 cups quartered cherry tomatoes

1/4 cup finely chopped parsley

2 tablespoons lemon juice

1/2 cup grated Parmesan cheese

Cook pasta according to package directions; drain. Meanwhile, warm oil in a large skillet over medium heat. Add onion and garlic. Sauté for 3 minutes. Add beans, broth, sage, oregano, basil, salt, and pepper. Cook for 5 minutes, stirring often, and mashing some of the beans to thicken sauce. Stir in tomatoes, parsley, and lemon juice. Heat through. Toss pasta with tomato-bean sauce and cheese; serve immediately.

PREPARATION TIME:
15 MINUTES

COOKING TIME:
25 MINUTES

NUTRIENT INFORMATION
(PER SERVING):

SERVINGS PER RECIPE:	8
SERVING SIZE:	1 CUP
CALORIES	249
PROTEIN	12 G.
CARBOHYDRATE	39 G.
FAT	5 G.
SATURATED FAT	2 G.
CHOLESTEROL	5 MG.
SODIUM	206 MG.
DIETARY FIBER	3 G.

% CALORIES FROM:

PROTEIN:	19%
CARBOHYDRATE:	63%
FAT:	18%

FOOD EXCHANGES:

2 STARCH

1 LEAN MEAT

1 VEGETABLE

MAKES 8 SERVINGS.

Garbanzo and Black Bean Curry

PREPARATION TIME:
15 MINUTES

COOKING TIME:
15 MINUTES

NUTRIENT INFORMATION
(PER SERVING):
SERVINGS PER RECIPE: 8
SERVING SIZE: 1/2 CUP
CALORIES   163
PROTEIN   8 G.
CARBOHYDRATE   26 G.
FAT   3 G.
SATURATED FAT   <1 G.
CHOLESTEROL   0 MG.
SODIUM   208 MG.
DIETARY FIBER   6 G.

% CALORIES FROM:
PROTEIN: 20%
CARBOHYDRATE: 64%
FAT: 16%

FOOD EXCHANGES:
1 STARCH
2 VEGETABLE

MAKES 8 SERVINGS.

A taste of curry turns this side dish into the centerpiece of the meal!

2 teaspoons canola oil

1 cup chopped onion

1/2 teaspoon ginger

2 teaspoons curry powder

15 1/2-ounce can no-added-salt tomatoes

1/8 teaspoon salt

1/4 teaspoon rosemary

15-ounce can black beans, rinsed and drained

15-ounce can garbanzo beans, rinsed and drained

1/3 cup chopped fresh parsley

1 tablespoon lemon juice

Heat oil in a large nonstick skillet over medium heat. Add onion, and sauté until tender. Stir in ginger and curry powder; cook an additional minute. Add tomatoes. Cook 1 minute or until mixture is slightly thickened, stirring occasionally. Add salt, rosemary, black beans, and garbanzo beans; stir well. Cover, reduce heat, and simmer 5 minutes. Remove from heat; stir in parsley and lemon juice.

Magic BEANS

Vegetable, Rice, and Lentil Pilaf

This tasty side dish is rich in complex carbohydrate, very low in fat, and satisfying when served with any variety of grilled meats.

Nonstick cooking spray

3/4 cup chopped onion

1/2 cup chopped celery

1/2 cup chopped green bell pepper

1/2 cup sliced fresh mushrooms

1 cup water

1/2 cup lentils, uncooked

1/2 teaspoon garlic powder

16-ounce can low-sodium chicken broth

2/3 cup uncooked brown rice

Coat a saucepan with cooking spray. Place over medium heat until hot. Add onion, celery, pepper, and mushrooms. Sauté 3 minutes or until tender. Add water, lentils, garlic powder, and chicken broth, and bring to a boil. Cook 2 minutes. Cover, reduce heat, and simmer 20 minutes. Add rice; simmer 20 minutes or until rice is done and lentils are tender. Stir well and serve.

PREPARATION TIME:
5 MINUTES

COOKING TIME:
45 MINUTES

NUTRIENT INFORMATION
(PER SERVING):

SERVINGS PER RECIPE:	8
SERVING SIZE:	1/2 CUP
CALORIES	105
PROTEIN	4 G.
CARBOHYDRATE	21 G.
FAT	<1 G.
SATURATED FAT	<1 G.
CHOLESTEROL	0 MG.
SODIUM	27 MG.
DIETARY FIBER	1 G.

% CALORIES FROM:

PROTEIN:	15%
CARBOHYDRATE:	80%
FAT:	5%

FOOD EXCHANGES:
1 STARCH
1 VEGETABLE

MAKES 8 SERVINGS.

Lively Lima Beans

PREPARATION TIME:
10 MINUTES

COOKING TIME:
20 MINUTES

NUTRIENT INFORMATION
(PER SERVING):
SERVINGS PER RECIPE: 8
SERVING SIZE: 1/2 CUP
CALORIES   61
PROTEIN   3 G.
CARBOHYDRATE   11 G.
FAT   <1 G.
SATURATED FAT   <1 G.
CHOLESTEROL   0 MG.
SODIUM   276 MG.
DIETARY FIBER   3 G.

% CALORIES FROM:
PROTEIN: 20%
CARBOHYDRATE: 72%
FAT: 8%

FOOD EXCHANGES:
2 VEGETABLE

MAKES 8 SERVINGS.

These spicy lima beans make a colorful low-fat side dish!

Nonstick cooking spray
1/2 cup chopped celery
1/2 cup chopped onion
1/2 cup chopped red pepper
10-ounce package frozen lima beans, thawed
10-ounce can chopped tomatoes with green chiles, undrained
1 cup vegetable juice
1/4 teaspoon basil
1 bay leaf

Coat a large nonstick skillet with cooking spray; place over medium-high heat until hot. Sauté celery, onion, and pepper 3 to 5 minutes or until crisp-tender. Add remaining ingredients. Mix well. Bring to a boil. Cover, reduce heat, and simmer 12 minutes, or until lima beans are tender, stirring occasionally. Discard bay leaf before serving.

Magic BEANS

Mideastern Garbanzo Beans

This exotic side dish which can be served as a meatless main dish if portion sizes are increased and it's served over rice.

1 tablespoon canola oil
1 large onion, sliced
1 medium onion, chopped
1 clove garlic, minced
1 cup diced acorn squash
1/4 cup golden raisins
1 cup low-sodium chicken broth
1 teaspoon rosemary
1 teaspoon cinnamon
1/2 teaspoon ginger
15-ounce can garbanzo beans, rinsed and drained

Heat oil in a 3-quart saucepan over medium heat. Cook sliced onion, chopped onion, and garlic in oil about 7 minutes until onions are tender. Stir in remaining ingredients except garbanzo beans. Heat to boiling; reduce heat. Cover and simmer about 8 minutes, stirring occasionally, until squash is tender. Stir in beans; heat through.

PREPARATION TIME:
10 MINUTES

COOKING TIME:
25 MINUTES

NUTRIENT INFORMATION
(PER SERVING):
SERVINGS PER RECIPE: 8
SERVING SIZE: 1/2 CUP
CALORIES   111
PROTEIN   4 G.
CARBOHYDRATE   17 G.
FAT   3 G.
SATURATED FAT   <1 G.
CHOLESTEROL   0 MG.
SODIUM   196 MG.
DIETARY FIBER   3 G.

% CALORIES FROM:
PROTEIN: 14%
CARBOHYDRATE: 62%
FAT: 24%

FOOD EXCHANGES:
1 STARCH
1 FAT

MAKES 8 SERVINGS.

Heart of Dixie Baked Beans

PREPARATION TIME:
10 MINUTES

COOKING TIME:
25 MINUTES

NUTRIENT INFORMATION
(PER SERVING):

SERVINGS PER RECIPE:	10
SERVING SIZE:	1 CUP
CALORIES	293
PROTEIN	10 G.
CARBOHYDRATE	61 G.
FAT	1 G.
SATURATED FAT	<1 G.
CHOLESTEROL	0 MG.
SODIUM	604 MG.
DIETARY FIBER	13 G.

% CALORIES FROM:

PROTEIN:	14%
CARBOHYDRATE:	83%
FAT:	3%

FOOD EXCHANGES:
4 STARCH

MAKES 10 SERVINGS.

Baked beans prepared "southern-style"!

Nonstick cooking spray
2 tablespoons water
1/4 cup chopped green bell pepper
2 medium onions, chopped
1 cup firmly packed brown sugar
2 tablespoons prepared mustard
15-ounce can no-added-salt stewed tomatoes, undrained
1 tablespoon cider vinegar
15-ounce can light red kidney beans, rinsed and drained
3 15-ounce cans vegetarian baked beans

Coat a medium skillet with cooking spray; add water. Sauté green pepper and onions until water has evaporated and pepper and onions are tender. Stir in remaining ingredients. Cover and simmer 20 minutes.

Magic BEANS

Tropical Baked Beans

Fruit salad, prunes, and mango chutney are some of the unusual ingredients that give this baked bean dish a tropical twist!

8-ounces Italian turkey sausage, casing removed

1 1/2 cups jicama, cut into 1/2-inch cubes

15 1/4-ounce can tropical fruit salad, drained

15-ounce can red beans, rinsed and drained

15-ounce can black beans, rinsed and drained

15-ounce can navy beans, rinsed and drained

14-ounce can no-added-salt diced tomatoes, undrained

1/2 cup coarsely chopped pitted prunes

1/2 cup mango chutney

3 tablespoons cider vinegar

2 teaspoons ground cumin

1/2 teaspoon allspice

1/2 teaspoon red pepper flakes

Cook sausage in a small skillet over medium heat 5 to 7 minutes or until browned. Drain thoroughly on paper towels, and crumble. Drain fat from skillet; add jicama, and sauté until it starts to brown, about 5 minutes. Mix all ingredients in a 2 1/2-quart casserole. Bake, covered, at 350° for 30 minutes.

PREPARATION TIME:
10 MINUTES

COOKING TIME:
40 MINUTES

NUTRIENT INFORMATION
(PER SERVING):

SERVINGS PER RECIPE:	12
SERVING SIZE:	1 CUP
CALORIES	292
PROTEIN	14 G.
CARBOHYDRATE	50 G.
FAT	4 G.
SATURATED FAT	1 G.
CHOLESTEROL	15 MG.
SODIUM	143 MG.
DIETARY FIBER	7 G.

% CALORIES FROM:

PROTEIN:	19%
CARBOHYDRATE:	68%
FAT:	12%

FOOD EXCHANGES:
2 STARCH
1 LEAN MEAT
1 VEGETABLE
1 FRUIT

MAKES 12 SERVINGS.

Peppery Beans With Tortilla Toppers

PREPARATION TIME:
15 MINUTES

COOKING TIME:
25 MINUTES

NUTRIENT INFORMATION
(PER SERVING):

SERVINGS PER RECIPE:	8
SERVING SIZE:	3/4 CUP
CALORIES	208
PROTEIN	10 G.
CARBOHYDRATE	33 G.
FAT	4 G.
SATURATED FAT	1 G.
CHOLESTEROL	0 MG.
SODIUM	27 MG.
DIETARY FIBER	7 G.

% CALORIES FROM:

PROTEIN:	19%
CARBOHYDRATE:	64%
FAT:	16%

FOOD EXCHANGES:
2 STARCH
1 VEGETABLE
1 FAT

MAKES 8 SERVINGS.

Bright colors and a zesty flavor make this a favorite. Tortilla strips on top are a change of pace from the usual side dish.

1 tablespoon plus 2 teaspoons olive oil

2 corn tortillas, cut into 1/2-inch strips

1 cup chopped onion

1 red bell pepper, cut into strips

1 green bell pepper, cut into strips

1 cup broccoli florets

16-ounce can red kidney beans, rinsed and drained

16-ounce can black beans, rinsed and drained

2 tablespoons no-added-salt tomato paste

1 teaspoon low-sodium Worcestershire sauce

1/2 teaspoon ground cumin

2 tablespoons chopped fresh cilantro

2 tablespoons lime juice

In a large nonstick skillet, warm 1 tablespoon of the olive oil over medium heat. Add tortilla strips; cook, turning strips once, until golden (3 to 4 minutes). Remove from the pan, and blot with paper towels. In the same pan, heat the remaining 2 teaspoons of olive oil. Add the onions, peppers, and broccoli; stir-fry until vegetables are crisp-tender, about 2 minutes. Stir in the kidney beans, black beans, tomato paste, Worcestershire sauce, and cumin; cover and simmer until the flavors blend, 10 to 15 minutes. Stir in the cilantro and lime juice. Sprinkle each serving with tortilla strips.

Magic BEANS

Sweet and Sour Pintos

This side dish could easily become a main dish if served over rice. It's a wonderful substitute for the traditional high-fat versions of sweet and sour chicken or pork.

20-ounce can unsweetened pineapple chunks

1/4 cup firmly packed brown sugar

2 tablespoons cornstarch

1/4 cup vinegar

1 tablespoon low-sodium soy sauce

1/4 cup low-sodium chicken broth

16-ounce can pinto beans, rinsed and drained

1 medium green bell pepper, chopped

1 small onion, minced

Drain pineapple, reserving juice. In a medium saucepan, combine brown sugar and cornstarch. Add reserved pineapple juice, vinegar, soy sauce, and chicken broth. Cook, stirring frequently, over medium heat until thick and bubbly, about 5 minutes. Remove from heat; add beans, pineapple, green pepper, and onion. Cook over medium heat for 10 minutes or until vegetables are crisp-tender.

PREPARATION TIME:
10 MINUTES

COOKING TIME:
15 MINUTES

NUTRIENT INFORMATION
(PER SERVING):
SERVINGS PER RECIPE: 6
SERVING SIZE: 3/4 CUP
CALORIES   209
PROTEIN   7 G.
CARBOHYDRATE   43 G.
FAT   1 G.
SATURATED FAT   <1 G.
CHOLESTEROL   0 MG.
SODIUM   99 MG.
DIETARY FIBER   7 G.

% CALORIES FROM:
PROTEIN: 13%
CARBOHYDRATE: 82%
FAT: 4%

FOOD EXCHANGES:
2 STARCH
1 FRUIT

MAKES 6 SERVINGS.

Spanish Salsa

PREPARATION TIME:
15 MINUTES

CHILLING TIME:
30 MINUTES

NUTRIENT INFORMATION
(PER SERVING):

SERVINGS PER RECIPE:	12
SERVING SIZE:	1/4 CUP
CALORIES	66
PROTEIN	3 G.
CARBOHYDRATE	9 G.
FAT	2 G.
SATURATED FAT	<1 G.
CHOLESTEROL	0 MG.
SODIUM	81 MG.
DIETARY FIBER	1 G.

% CALORIES FROM:

PROTEIN:	18%
CARBOHYDRATE:	55%
FAT:	27%

FOOD EXCHANGES:
2 VEGETABLE

MAKES 12 SERVINGS.

Salsa adds a delicious finishing touch to main dishes such as grilled beef, fish, or chicken. This black bean salsa also makes a great filling for tortillas!

15-ounce can black beans, rinsed and drained
1/2 cup diced red bell pepper
1/2 cup diced green bell pepper
1/4 cup purple onion, minced
1/4 cup diced unpeeled cucumber
2 tablespoons canned chopped green chiles, drained
1 tablespoon fresh basil
1 tablespoon plus 2 teaspoons olive oil
3 tablespoons tomato juice
2 tablespoons red wine vinegar
1 tablespoon lime juice
1 teaspoon fresh thyme
1/2 teaspoon ground cumin
1/2 teaspoon chili powder
1/4 teaspoon salt
1/4 teaspoon black pepper
1 clove garlic, minced

Combine all ingredients in a bowl. Stir well. Cover and chill at least 30 minutes.

Magic BEANS

Lentil Citrus Salsa

This unusual salsa can be paired with dishes such as pork tenderloin or grilled chicken.

2 cups lentils, uncooked

1 1/2 quarts water

1 1/2 teaspoons ground cumin

1 cup orange juice

1/4 cup lime juice

1 cup diced red onion

1/4 cup chopped fresh cilantro

1/2 cup minced scallions

1 tomato, seeded and chopped

1 clove garlic, minced

Dressing:

2 tablespoons thawed orange juice concentrate

3 tablespoons olive oil

1/2 teaspoon dry mustard

1/2 teaspoon chili powder

1/4 teaspoon ground cumin

Simmer the lentils in water with cumin for 15 minutes, or until tender. Drain. Add orange juice, lime juice, and onion. Toss gently, and chill for 8 hours. Drain. Gently stir in cilantro, scallions, tomato, and garlic. Combine the dressing ingredients, and pour over the lentil mixture. Toss gently. Refrigerate for at least 30 minutes.

PREPARATION TIME:
10 MINUTES

COOKING TIME:
15 MINUTES

CHILLING TIME:
8 1/2 HOURS

NUTRIENT INFORMATION
(PER SERVING):

SERVINGS PER RECIPE:	10
SERVING SIZE:	1/4 CUP
CALORIES	136
PROTEIN	5 G.
CARBOHYDRATE	20 G.
FAT	4 G.
SATURATED FAT	1 G.
CHOLESTEROL	0 MG.
SODIUM	15 MG.
DIETARY FIBER	2 G.

% CALORIES FROM:

PROTEIN:	15%
CARBOHYDRATE:	59%
FAT:	26%

FOOD EXCHANGES:
1 STARCH
1 VEGETABLE
1 FAT

MAKES 10 SERVINGS.

BRAVE-HEARTED
BEAN LOVER

*Unique
Bean
Recipes*

Blueberry Bean Muffins

This delicious recipe is an adaptation of a winner from America's Best Bean Recipe Contest. I've included it especially for those who don't think it's possible to eat beans for breakfast.

2 15-ounce cans red kidney beans, rinsed and drained

1/3 cup skim milk

1 cup sugar

1/4 cup diet margarine, softened

3/4 cup egg substitute (equal to 3 eggs)

2 teaspoons vanilla

1 cup flour

1/2 cup whole wheat flour

1 teaspoon baking soda

1/2 teaspoon salt

1 teaspoon cinnamon

1/2 teaspoon allspice

1/2 teaspoon cloves

1 cup fresh or frozen blueberries

3/4 cup chopped pecans

In a food processor or blender, process beans and milk until smooth. In a large bowl, mix sugar and margarine; beat in egg substitute and vanilla. Add bean mixture, mixing until well blended. Mix in combined flours, baking soda, salt, cinnamon, allspice, and cloves. Gently mix in blueberries. Spoon mixture into greased or paper-lined muffin cups. Sprinkle with pecans. Bake muffins in a preheated 375° oven until toothpick inserted in center comes out clean, 20 to 25 minutes. Cool in pan on wire racks 5 minutes.

PREPARATION TIME:
20 MINUTES

BAKING TIME:
25 MINUTES

NUTRIENT INFORMATION
(PER SERVING):

SERVINGS PER RECIPE:	14
SERVING SIZE:	1 MUFFIN
CALORIES	271
PROTEIN	8 G.
CARBOHYDRATE	44 G.
FAT	7 G.
SATURATED FAT	1 G.
CHOLESTEROL	<1 MG.
SODIUM	271 MG.
DIETARY FIBER	5 G.

% CALORIES FROM:

PROTEIN:	12%
CARBOHYDRATE:	65%
FAT:	23%

FOOD EXCHANGES:
3 STARCH
1 FAT

MAKES 14 MUFFINS.

Chocolate Lover's Lentil Brownies

PREPARATION TIME:
15 MINUTES

COOKING TIME:
40 MINUTES

BAKING TIME:
35 MINUTES

NUTRIENT INFORMATION
(PER SERVING):

SERVINGS PER RECIPE:	24
SERVING SIZE:	1 BROWNIE
CALORIES	197
PROTEIN	3 G.
CARBOHYDRATE	35 G.
FAT	5 G.
SATURATED FAT	<1 G.
CHOLESTEROL	<1 MG.
SODIUM	114 MG.
DIETARY FIBER	2 G.

% CALORIES FROM:

PROTEIN:	6%
CARBOHYDRATE:	71%
FAT:	23%

FOOD EXCHANGES:
1 VEGETABLE
2 FRUIT
1 FAT

MAKES 2 DOZEN
BROWNIES.

Lentils provide the chewy texture for this low-fat brownie recipe. Applesauce is a great substitute for oil!

1/2 cup lentils, uncooked
1 1/2 cups water
1 cup egg substitute (equal to 4 eggs)
1 3/4 cups sugar
1/4 cup corn oil
3/4 cup applesauce
2 teaspoons vanilla
1 1/2 cups whole wheat flour
1/2 cup plus 2 tablespoons cocoa
1/2 teaspoon salt
1/2 cup chocolate chips
1 cup marshmallows
Nonstick cooking spray

Rinse the lentils, and combine with water in a pan. Bring to a boil. Reduce the heat, cover, and simmer for 40 minutes or until tender. Drain off the excess liquid.

In the meantime, beat the egg substitute and sugar. Add the oil, applesauce, vanilla, flour, cocoa, and salt to the sugar and egg substitute mixture. Stir in the cooked lentils, chocolate chips, and marshmallows. Press into a 9" x 13" pan coated with cooking spray. Bake for 35 minutes at 350°. Cool, and cut.

Magic BEANS

Dreamy Bean Bars

These bars were adapted from a recipe from the Bavarian Inn in Frankenmuth, Michigan.

Crust:

2/3 cup canned cannellini beans, rinsed and drained

1/3 cup diet margarine

1/2 cup firmly packed brown sugar

3/4 cup whole wheat flour

Nonstick cooking spray

In a medium mixing bowl, blend beans, margarine, brown sugar, and flour. Press mixture into the bottom of an 8" x 8" pan coated with cooking spray. Bake at 350° for 20 minutes; remove from oven, and cool slightly.

Filling:

1/2 cup canned cannellini beans, rinsed and drained

1/2 cup egg substitute (equal to 2 eggs)

2/3 cup sugar

1/2 cup finely chopped walnuts

3/4 cup coconut

1 teaspoon vanilla

1/4 cup mini chocolate chips

Mix all ingredients in a medium bowl until well blended. Spread mixture on top of crust. Bake for 30 minutes at 350°. Cool. Cut into squares.

PREPARATION TIME:
20 MINUTES

BAKING TIME:
50 MINUTES

NUTRIENT INFORMATION
(PER SERVING):

SERVINGS PER RECIPE:	16
SERVING SIZE:	1 BAR
CALORIES	173
PROTEIN	3 G.
CARBOHYDRATE	29 G.
FAT	5 G.
SATURATED FAT	2 G.
CHOLESTEROL	1 MG.
SODIUM	71 MG.
DIETARY FIBER	1 G.

% CALORIES FROM:

PROTEIN:	7%
CARBOHYDRATE:	67%
FAT:	26%

FOOD EXCHANGES:
1 STARCH
1 FRUIT
1 FAT

MAKES 16 BARS.

Raisin Spice Lentil Cookies

PREPARATION TIME:
20 MINUTES

COOKING TIME:
40 MINUTES

BAKING TIME:
10 MINUTES

NUTRIENT INFORMATION
(PER SERVING):

SERVINGS PER RECIPE: 36
SERVING SIZE: 1 COOKIE
CALORIES   82
PROTEIN   3 G.
CARBOHYDRATE   13 G.
FAT   2 G.
SATURATED FAT   <1 G.
CHOLESTEROL   <1 MG.
SODIUM   54 MG.
DIETARY FIBER   1 G.

% CALORIES FROM:

PROTEIN: 15%
CARBOHYDRATE: 63%
FAT: 22%

FOOD EXCHANGES:
1 STARCH

MAKES 3 DOZEN
COOKIES.

These cookies fill the kitchen with a delicious fragrance while baking. They taste great fresh from the oven with a glass of cold skim milk.

3/4 cup lentils, uncooked

1 1/2 cups water

1/2 cup egg substitute (equal to 2 eggs)

1/2 cup honey

1/4 cup diet margarine

1 teaspoon vanilla

1/3 cup canned pumpkin

1/2 cup unbleached flour

1 1/2 cups whole wheat flour

1/4 teaspoon salt

1 teaspoons baking powder

1 teaspoon cinnamon

1/4 teaspoon nutmeg

1/4 teaspoon ginger

1/4 teaspoon orange peel

1 cup coarsely chopped walnuts

1/2 cup raisins

Nonstick cooking spray

Rinse lentils, and combine with water in a pan. Bring to a boil. Reduce the heat, cover, and simmer for 40 minutes or until tender. Drain off excess liquid.

In the meantime, beat the egg substitute in a medium bowl. Add the honey and margarine. Cream until smooth. Add the vanilla, pumpkin, and cooked lentils. In a large bowl, combine the flours, salt, baking powder, cinnamon, nutmeg, ginger, and orange peel. Add the lentil mixture, and mix well. Fold in walnuts and raisins.

Drop the dough by rounded tablespoons onto a cookie sheet sprayed with cooking spray. Bake for 10 minutes at 350°.

Magic BEANS

Fruit and Spice Pinto Bean Cake

This moist cake is packed with good nutrition, as well as good taste!

Nonstick cooking spray

2 cups canned pinto beans, rinsed and drained

1/4 cup egg substitute (equal to 1 egg)

1/4 cup diet margarine, melted

1 cup flour

1 teaspoon baking soda

1/4 teaspoon salt

1 teaspoon cinnamon

1 teaspoon allspice

1/2 teaspoon cloves

2 cups chopped Granny Smith apples

1/4 cup finely chopped walnuts

1 cup golden raisins

2 teaspoons vanilla extract

1/4 cup powdered sugar

Preheat oven to 375°. Spray a 10-inch tube pan with cooking spray. In a food processor, puree the beans, egg substitute, and melted margarine. In a medium bowl, mix the flour, baking soda, salt, cinnamon, allspice, and cloves. Blend dry ingredients into bean mixture using several on and off motions of food processor until well combined. Scrape batter into a mixing bowl, and add apples, walnuts, raisins, and vanilla. Stir until well blended. Pour into tube pan, and bake in center of oven for 50 minutes. Turn upside down onto wire rack to cool. Dust with powdered sugar.

PREPARATION TIME:
20 MINUTES

BAKING TIME:
50 MINUTES

NUTRIENT INFORMATION
(PER SERVING):
SERVINGS PER RECIPE: 10
SERVING SIZE: 1/10 OF CAKE
CALORIES   208
PROTEIN   6 G.
CARBOHYDRATE   37 G.
FAT   4 G.
SATURATED FAT   1 G.
CHOLESTEROL   0 MG.
SODIUM   246 MG.
DIETARY FIBER   4 G.

% CALORIES FROM:
PROTEIN: 12%
CARBOHYDRATE: 71%
FAT: 17%

FOOD EXCHANGES:
2 STARCH
1 VEGETABLE
1 FAT

MAKES 1 CAKE.

Black Bean Corn Bread

PREPARATION TIME:
15 MINUTES

BAKING TIME:
50 MINUTES

NUTRIENT INFORMATION
(PER SERVING):

SERVINGS PER RECIPE: 16
SERVING SIZE: 1 SQUARE
CALORIES   178
PROTEIN   6 G.
CARBOHYDRATE   25 G.
FAT   6 G.
SATURATED FAT   1 G.
CHOLESTEROL   4 MG.
SODIUM   373 MG.
DIETARY FIBER   2 G.

% CALORIES FROM:
PROTEIN: 13%
CARBOHYDRATE: 56%
FAT: 30%

FOOD EXCHANGES:
2 STARCH
1 FAT

MAKES 16 SQUARES.

This spicy corn bread goes well with chili or a hearty bean soup.

Nonstick cooking spray
3 cups Bisquick baking mix
1 cup cornmeal
3/4 cup canned black beans, rinsed and drained
3/4 cup shredded low-fat cheddar cheese
1 cup skim milk
1 cup egg substitute (equal to 4 eggs)
2 tablespoons canola oil
1/2 teaspoon chili powder
1/8 teaspoon ground cumin
1/2 teaspoon oregano
2 medium tomatoes, seeded and finely chopped
4-ounce can diced green chiles, drained

Preheat oven to 375°. Spray bottom only of a 9" x 9" pan with cooking spray; dust with flour. Mix all ingredients; beat 30 strokes. Spread in pan. Bake 50 minutes or until toothpick inserted in center comes out clean. Cool 5 minutes. Cut into squares, and serve warm.

Magic BEANS

Bibliography

Anderson, J.W. *Plant Fiber in Foods*. Lexington, KY: HCF Nutrition Research Foundation, 1990.

Exchange Lists for Meal Planning. The American Dietetic Association and The American Diabetes Association, 1995.

Food Values of Portions Commonly Used (16th edition). Philadelphia, PA: JB Lippincott, 1993.

Geil, PB and Anderson, J.W. *Nutrition and Health Implications of Dry Beans: A Review*. Journal of the American College of Nutrition 13: 549-558, 1994.

Lentil and Split Pea Cookbook. Seattle, WA: Peanut Butter Press, 1990.

Stone, S. and Stone, M. *The Brilliant Bean*. New York, NY: Bantam Books, 1988.

USDA: The Food Guide Pyramid, 1992.

USDA and USDHHS: *Dietary Guidelines for Americans*, 1995.

Index

Anne's Lemony Lentil Soup, 58
Appetizer Black Bean Burritos, 27
appetizers, 20-40
artichoke heart medley, black bean pasta
  and, 158

bake, turkey bean, 108
baked beans,
  bang-up Boston, 160
  heart of Dixie, 168
  Tex-Mex, 155
  tropical, 169
Bang-Up Boston Baked Beans, 160
Barley and Black Bean Salad, 89
bars, dreamy bean, 179
Basic Beef and Vegetable Chili, 54
Bean and Orzo Salad, 82
Bean Submarine Salad, 85
bean
  and pasta stew, Irene's zesty, 44
  burritos, beefy, 105
  dip with crispy tortilla chips, zippy, 39
bean dip,
  black, 32
  Italian, 28
  layered ranch and, 29
  southwest, 37
  spicy surprise, 38
  turkey taco, 40
bean measurements, 16

bean soup,
  economy and hominy, 63
  peanutty, 47
  simple white, 48
bean spread, cannellini, 33
bean stew, taco, 52
bean storage, 15
Beano, 17
beans and rice,
  robust, 144
  speedy spicy, 153
beans,
  canned, IX
  cooking, 13-16
  health benefits of, VII-VIII, 9-11
  history of, 1
  rinsing, 13
  serving suggestions, 5-6
  shopping for, 13
  soaking, 13-14
  sodium content, IX
beef and vegetable chili, basic, 54
Beefy Bean Burritos, 105
Best Black Bean and Rice Burritos, 119
Best-of-the-West Pasta Salad, 97
Black and White Salad, 71
Black Bean and Red Cabbage Slaw, 76
Black Bean Corn Bread, 182
Black Bean Dip, 32
Black Bean Gazpacho, 53

Black Bean Pasta and Artichoke Heart
    Medley, 158
Black Bean Pizza, 146
Black Bean Summer Salad, 93
Black Bean Sweet Potato Turkey Salad,
    104
black bean
    and rice burritos, best, 119
    burritos, appetizer, 27
    chili, lamb and, 60
    curry, garbanzo and, 164
black bean recipes,
    appetizers, 22, 27, 32, 36
    main dishes, 104, 111, 118-119, 123,
        129, 132, 135-136, 138, 145-146, 148-
        149
    salads, 71, 76, 78, 82, 87, 89, 93, 97
    side dishes, 156, 158, 164, 169-170, 172
    soups and chilis, 53, 57, 60
    unique, 182
black bean salad,
    barley and, 89
    south-of-the-border, 87
    sunshine, 78
    souperior, 57
black beans and rice,
    confetti, 156
    tropical, 111
black beans, 5, 7
    island chicken with, 135
Black-Eyed Chicken Salad, 106
Black-Eyed Pea Salsa, 35
Black-Eyed Peas on the Side, 157
black-eyed pea
    dip, party time, 31
    salad, make-ahead, 74
black-eyed pea recipes,
    appetizers, 21, 25, 31, 35

main dishes, 106, 133
    salads, 67, 74
    side dishes, 157
black-eyed peas, 5, 7
blood sugar, 10
Blue Ribbon Bean Enchiladas, 128
Blueberry Bran Muffins, 177
Boston baked beans, bang-up, 160
bran muffins, blueberry, 177
bread, black bean corn, 182
brownies, chocolate lover's lentil, 178
burgers, where's-the-beef, 134
burritos,
    appetizer black bean, 27
    beefy bean, 105
    best black bean and rice, 119
    garden, 127
butter beans, 6

cabbage slaw, black bean and red, 76
cake, fruit and spice pinto bean, 181
calcium content, beans, 4
calorie content, beans, 2
cancer, 10
canned beans, IX
Cannellini Bean Spread, 33
cannellini bean recipes,
    appetizers, 26, 33
    main dishes, 126
    salads, 88, 90
    side dishes, 154, 162-163
    soups and chilis, 45, 51
    unique, 179
cannellini beans, 5, 7
cannellini, citrus, 162
carbohydrate, beans, 3
casserole,
    Coronado, 114

Magic BEANS

lamb and lentil, 121
   Mexitalian, 132
   microwave taco, 102
cassoulet, shortcut, 118
caviar, faux, 21
ceci beans, 5
Cheesy Bean Quiche, 137
chick-pea
   dip, peppery, 34
   pasta salad, orange, 86
chicken
   chili, tipsy, 46
   salad, black-eyed, 106
   with black beans, island, 135
chicken,
   fiesta, 123
   rush hour, 145
chickpeas, 5
chili
   bean salad, Tex-Mex, 68
   macaroni, favorite, 107
   recipes, 43, 46, 49, 54, 56, 60, 64
chili,
   basic beef and vegetable, 54
   Crockpot vegetable, 49
   fruit and nut, 56
   lamb and black bean, 60
   shortcut vegetarian, 43
   Tami's white, 64
   tipsy chicken, 46
Chilled Tuna Bean Salad, 126
Chocolate Lover's Lentil Brownies, 178
cholesterol content, beans, 3
cholesterol-lowering benefits, 9-10
chronic diseases, 3-4, 9-11
Citrus Cannellini, 162
citrus salsa, lentil, 173

Confetti Black Beans and Rice, 156
Confetti Paella, 109
cookies, raisin spice lentil, 180
cooking
   beans, 13-16
     in Crockpot, 15
     in microwave, 14-15
     in pressure cooker, 14
   lentils, 15
   split peas, 15
Cool Lentil Salad, 88
copper content, beans, 4
corn bread, black bean, 182
Coronado Casserole, 114
cowpeas, 5
Crockpot Vegetable Chili, 49
Crowd-Pleasing Chunky Minestrone, 51
Crunchy Rainbow Lentil Salad, 98
Curried Lentils With Fruit, 159
curry, garbanzo and black bean, 164

desserts, 178-181
diabetes, 10
Dietary Guidelines for Americans, 9, 11
Dijon bean salad, warm, 80
dip with crispy tortilla chips, zippy bean, 39
dip,
   black bean, 32
   hummus, 24
   Italian bean, 28
   layered ranch and bean, 29
   lively lentil, 30
   party time black-eyed pea, 31
   peppery chick-pea, 34
   savory white bean, 26
   southwest bean, 37
   spicy surprise bean, 38

INDEX

take-five, 22
turkey taco bean, 40
dips, 22-24, 26, 28-32, 34-40, 172
Down-Home Hummus, 25
Dreamy Bean Bars, 179

Economy Hominy and Bean Soup, 63
enchiladas, blue ribbon bean, 128

fat content, beans, 3-4
Faux Caviar, 21
fava beans, 5, 7
Favorite Chili Macaroni, 107
Festive Lentil Toss, 92
Fettuccine With Hot Mexican Bean Sauce,
    122
fiber content, beans, 3
Fiesta Chicken, 123
Fiesta Potato Salad, 79
Firehouse Lentil Soup, 50
flatulence, 16-17
folacin content, beans, 4
Food Pyramid Guide, 11
Four-Bean Salad, 75
freezing beans, 16
Fruit and Nut Chili, 56
Fruit and Spice Pinto Bean Cake, 181
fruit, curried lentils with, 159

Garbanzo and Black Bean Curry, 164
Garbanzo Guac, 23
Garbanzo Salad, 72
garbanzo bean recipes,
    appetizers, 23-24, 34
    main dishes, 109, 137, 140
    salads, 68-69, 70, 72, 75, 81, 85-86, 96
    side dishes, 150, 164, 167

soups and chilis, 43, 46-47
garbanzo beans, 5, 7
    mideastern, 167
Garden Burritos, 127
garden salad, Italian, 81
gas, bean-produced, 16-17
gazpacho, black bean, 53
Great Bean Gumbo, 131
Great Northern bean recipes, 28, 48, 63,
    75, 94
Great Northern beans, 5, 7
Greek Pasta Bean Salad, 91
Green Soybean Salad, 83
guacamole,
    garbanzo, 23
    shortcut, 36
gumbo, great bean, 131

haricot beans, 6
health benefits of beans, 9-11
Heart of Dixie Baked Beans, 168
heart disease, 9
Hearty Mexican Potatoes, 115
hominy and bean soup, economy, 63
Hoppin' John Salad, 67
Hoppin' John, 133
Hummus Dip, 24
hummus, down-home, 25

Irene's Zesty Bean and Pasta Stew, 44
iron content, beans, 4
Island Chicken With Black Beans, 135
Italian Bean Dip, 28
Italian Garden Salad, 81

jicama, 87

Kidney Bean Taco Salad, 95
kidney bean recipes,
    main dishes, 103, 107, 110, 115-116,
        118, 122, 125, 127, 131, 134, 137,
        141, 143, 147
    salads, 68, 75, 77, 80, 91, 94, 95
    side dishes, 153, 155, 168, 170
    soups and chilis, 43-44, 52, 54, 56
    unique, 177
kidney beans, 6, 7

Lamb and Black Bean Chili, 60
Lamb and Lentil Casserole, 121
lasagna,
    Mexibean, 143
    Popeye's bean, 110
Layered Ranch and Bean Dip, 29
legumes, definition of, 1
lemony lentil soup, Anne's, 58
Lentil Citrus Salsa, 173
Lentil One-Dish Dinner, 139
Lentil Pita Treat, 113
lentil
    brownies, chocolate lover's, 178
    casserole, lamb and, 121
    cookies, raisin spice, 180
    dip, lively, 30
    pilaf, vegetable rice and, 165
lentil recipes,
    appetizers, 30
    main dishes, 113, 121, 139
    salads, 73, 84, 88, 92, 98
    side dishes, 159, 173
    soups and chilis, 50, 58, 62
    unique, 178, 180
lentil salad,
    cool, 88

crunchy rainbow, 98
    Moroccan, 84
    saucy, 73
lentil soup,
    Anne's lemony, 58
    firehouse, 50
    silky, 62
lentil toss, festive, 92
lentils with fruit, curried, 159
lentils, 6, 7
    cooking, 15
lima bean recipes, 166
lima beans, 6, 7
    lively, 166
Lively Lentil Dip, 30
Lively Lima Beans, 166
Lucky 13 Marinated Beans, 161

macaroni, favorite chili, 107
magnesium content, beans, 4
main dishes, 101-150
Make-Ahead Black-Eyed Pea Salad, 74
manicotti, Mexican microwave, 124
marinated beans, lucky 13, 161
measuring beans, 16
Mediterranean Bean Salad, 69
Mediterranean Pocket Sandwiches, 140
Mexibean Lasagna, 143
Mexican bean sauce, fettuccine with hot,
    122
Mexican Microwave Manicotti, 124
Mexican potatoes, hearty, 115
Mexitalian Casserole, 132
Micro-Rave Red Beans and Rice, 117
Microwave Taco Casserole, 102
microwave manicotti, Mexican, 124
Mideastern Garbanzo Beans, 167

mineral content, beans, 4
minestrone, crowd-pleasing chunky, 51
Moroccan Lentil Salad, 84
muffins, blueberry bran, 177

navy bean recipes,
    main dishes, 118, 149
    salads, 64
    side dishes, 155, 160, 169
navy beans, 6, 8
    nutrition breakdown, 2
New Orleans Shrimp Soup, 59
niacin content, beans, 4
nut chili, fruit and, 56
nutrient analysis, IX
nutrition content of beans,
    calcium, 4
    calories, 2
    carbohydrate, 3
    copper, 4
    fat, 3-4
    folacin, 4
    iron, 4
    magnesium, 4
    minerals, 4
    niacin, 4
    phosphorus, 4
    potassium, 4
    protein, 2-3
    riboflavin, 4
    sodium, 4
    thiamin, 4
    vitamins, 4
    zinc, 4

obesity, 10
Old-Fashioned Pinto Bean Soup, 61
olé, rice skillet, 136

Olga's Garden Vegetables and Beans, 154
one-dish dinner,
    lentil, 139
    Spanish, 148
Orange Chick-Pea Pasta Salad, 86
Oriental Bean Toss, 94
orzo
    salad, bean and, 82
    skillet, turkey pinto, 120

paella, confetti, 109
Pam's Pita Tostadas, 138
Party Time Black-Eyed Pea Dip, 31
Pasta e Fagioli, 45
pasta
    and artichoke heart medley, black bean,
      158
    bean salad, Greek, 91
    salad,
      best-of-the-west, 97
      orange chick-pea, 86
    stew, Irene's zesty bean and, 44
    tomatoes and beans, red and white, 163
pea beans, 6
peanuts, fat content, 3
Peanutty Bean Soup, 47
Peppery Beans With Tortilla Toppers, 170
Peppery Chick-Pea Dip, 34
phosphorus content, beans, 4
phytochemicals, 10-11
pie, vegetable bean, 103
pilaf, vegetable rice and lentil, 165
pinto bean cake, fruit and spice, 181
pinto bean recipes,
    appetizers, 37-40
    main dishes, 101-102, 105, 112, 114,
      120, 124, 130, 144
    salads, 68, 79

Magic BEANS

side dishes, 155, 171
soups and chilis, 61
unique, 181
pinto bean soup, old-fashioned, 61
pinto beans, 6, 8
pinto orzo skillet, turkey, 120
Pinto-Packed Stuffed Peppers, 112
pintos, sweet and sour, 171
pita
 pizzas, pronto, 130
 tostadas, Pam's, 138
 treat, lentil, 113
pizza, black bean, 146
pizzas, pronto pita, 130
pocket sandwiches, Mediterranean, 140
Popeye's Bean Lasagna, 110
Pork Chops With Salsa Beans and Rice,
 147
potassium content, beans, 4
potato salad, fiesta, 79
potatoes, hearty Mexican, 115
potluck salad, veggie-bean, 77
Pronto Pita Pizzas, 130
protein content, beans, 3

quiche, cheesy bean, 137
Quick Bean Salad, 70

rainbow lentil salad, crunchy, 98
rainbows soup, red beans and, 55

Raisin Spice Lentil Cookies, 180
ranch and bean dip, layered, 29
Red and White Pasta Tomatoes and
 Beans, 163
Red Beans and Rainbows Soup, 55
red bean recipes,

main dishes, 117
side dishes, 169
soups and chilis, 55, 59
red beans and rice, micro-rave, 117
red beans, 6, 8
red cabbage slaw, black bean and, 76
refried bean recipes,
 appetizers, 29
 main dishes, 108, 128, 142
riboflavin content, beans, 4
Rice Skillet Olé, 136
rice
 and lentil pilaf, vegetable, 165
 burritos, best black bean and, 119
rice,
 confetti black beans and, 156
 micro-rave red beans and, 117
 pork chops with salsa beans and, 147
 robust beans and, 144
 speedy spicy beans and, 153
 tropical black beans and, 111
rinsing beans, 13, 17
Robust Beans and Rice, 144
Rush Hour Chicken, 145

salad,
 barley and black bean, 89
 bean and orzo, 82
 best-of-the-west pasta, 97
 black and white, 71
 black bean summer, 93
 black bean sweet potato turkey, 104
 black-eyed chicken, 106
 chilled tuna bean, 126
 cool lentil, 88
 crunchy rainbow lentil, 98
 festive lentil toss, 92

fiesta potato, 79
four-bean, 75
garbanzo, 72
Greek pasta bean, 91
green soybean, 83
hoppin' John, 67
Italian garden, 81
kidney bean taco, 95
make-ahead black-eyed pea, 74
Mediterranean bean, 69
Moroccan lentil, 84
orange chick-pea pasta, 86
Oriental bean toss, 94
quick bean, 70
saucy lentil, 73
seven-layer vegetable bean, 96
simply delicious white bean, 90
south-of-the-border black bean, 87
submarine bean, 85
sunshine black bean, 78
Tex-Mex chili bean, 68
veggie-bean potluck, 77
warm Dijon bean, 80
salads, 67-98, 106, 126
salsa
    beans and rice, pork chops with, 147
    sauté, turkey, 129
salsa,
    black-eyed pea, 35
    lentil citrus, 173
    Spanish, 172
sandwiches, Mediterranean pocket, 140
Santa Fe Stack-Ups, 101
sauce, fettucine with hot Mexican bean, 122
Saucy Lentil Salad, 73
sauté, turkey salsa, 129
Savory White Bean Dip, 26

serving suggestions, 5-6
Seven-Layer Vegetable Bean Salad, 96
shopping for beans, 13
Shortcut Cassoulet, 118
Shortcut Guacamole, 36
Shortcut Vegetarian Chili, 43
shrimp soup, New Orleans, 59
side dishes, 153-173
Silky Lentil Soup, 62
Simple White Bean Soup, 48
Simpy Delicious White Bean Salad, 90
skillet olé, rice, 136
slaw, black bean and red cabbage, 76
soaking beans, 13, 17
sodium content, beans, 4
soup,
    Anne's lemony lentil, 58
    economy hominy and bean, 63
    firehouse lentil, 50
    New Orleans shrimp, 59
    old-fashioned pinto bean, 61
    peanutty bean, 47
    red beans and rainbows, 55
    silky lentil, 62
    simple white bean, 48
    souperior black bean, 57
Souperior Black Bean Soup, 57
soup recipes, 44, 45, 47, 48, 50-53, 55, 57-59, 61-63
South-of-the-Border Black Bean Salad, 87
Southwest Bean Dip, 37
soybean
    recipes, 83
    salad, green, 83
soybeans, 3, 6, 8, 10
    fat content, 3
Spanish One-Dish Dinner, 148

Spanish Salsa, 172
Speedy Spicy Beans and Rice, 153
Spicy Surprise Bean Dip, 38
split peas, cooking, 15
spread, cannellini bean, 33
spreads, 21, 25, 33
stack-ups, Santa Fe, 101
stew,
    Irene's zesty bean and pasta, 44
    taco bean, 52
    vegetable, 116
storage, beans, 15
stuffed peppers, pinto-packed, 112
submarine salad, bean, 85
sugar content, beans, 3
summer salad, black bean, 93
Sunshine Black Bean Salad, 78
surprise bean dip, spicy, 38
Sweet and Sour Pintos, 171
sweet potato turkey salad, black bean, 104

Taco Bean Stew, 52
taco
    bean dip, turkey, 40
    casserole, microwave, 102
    salad, kidney bean, 95
taco-tico, turkey, 141
tahini, 24, 25
Take-Five Dip, 22
Tami's White Chili, 64
tater topper, turkey-bean, 149
Tex-Mex Baked Beans, 155
Tex-Mex Chili Bean Salad, 68
thiamin content, beans, 4
Time-Saver Tostadas, 125
Tipsy Chicken Chili, 46
tomatoes and beans, red and white pasta,
    163

tortilla toppers, peppery beans with, 170
tortillas, vegetarian, 142
tostadas,
    Pam's pita, 138
    time-saver, 125
    vegetable bean, 150
Tropical Baked Beans, 169
Tropical Black Beans and Rice, 111
tuna bean salad, chilled, 126
Turkey Bean Bake, 108
Turkey Salsa Sauté, 129
Turkey Taco Bean Dip, 40
Turkey Taco-Tico, 141
turkey salad, black bean sweet potato, 104
Turkey-Bean Tater Topper, 149
Turkey-Pinto-Orzo Skillet, 120
turtle beans, 5

Vegetable Bean Pie, 103
Vegetable Bean Tostadas, 150
Vegetable Rice and Lentil Pilaf, 165
Vegetable Stew, 116
vegetable
    bean salad, seven-layer, 96
    chili, basic beef and, 54
    chili, Crockpot, 49
vegetables and beans, Olga's garden, 154
Vegetarian Tortillas, 142
vegetarian
    chili, shortcut, 43
    diet, IX
Veggie-Bean Potluck Salad, 77
vitamin content, beans, 4

Warm Dijon Bean Salad, 80
weight loss, 10
Where's-the-Beef? Burgers, 134

INDEX

white bean
  dip, savory, 26
  salad, simply delicious, 90
  soup, simple, 48
white chili, Tami's, 64

zesty bean and pasta stew, Irene's, 44
zinc content, beans, 4
Zippy Bean Dip With Crispy Tortilla
  Chips, 39

Magic BEANS